ON DESIGN AND INNOVATION

THE RSA

The Royal Society for the encouragement of Arts, Manufactures and Commerce (RSA) was founded in 1754 with a mission to 'embolden enterprise, to enlarge science, to refine art, to improve our manufactures and to extend our commerce'. Believing that a thriving economy was the determining factor in the development of a civilized society, the RSA's founding Fellows sought to encourage innovation, the acquisition of new skills and the creation of new markets.

The RSA today uses its independence and the resources of its international Fellowship to stimulate debate, develop ideas and encourage action in its main fields of interest: business and industry, design and technology, education, the arts and the environment. The RSA Fellowship (now numbering nearly 21,500 in the UK and abroad) is drawn from almost every vocation and provides a resource of expertise and practical experience on which the Society can call.

The RSA is good at forming partnerships, at working with others to increase the pressure for change. The Society provides a forum for discussion within which ideas may be shaped and action stimulated. Often the process starts with a lecture, seminar or conference, then may follow active promotion through a project, campaign or award scheme.

Current projects include Redefining Schooling, PROJECT 2001, Focus on Food, Forum for Ethics in the Workplace, the RSA Student Design Awards, and The Arts Matter programme (see also the back pages of this book).

For more information please write to The Director, RSA, 8 John Adam Street, London WC2N 6EZ or telephone 0171 930 5115. (Fax 0171 839 5805, Website http://www.rsa.org.uk)

RSA

ON DESIGN
AND INNOVATION

*A selection of lectures organized by the
Royal Society for the encouragement of
Arts, Manufactures and Commerce*

Gower

Published by
Gower Publishing Limited
Gower House
Croft Road
Aldershot
Hampshire GU11 3HR
England

Gower
Old Post Road
Brookfield
Vermont 05036
USA

The authors of these lectures have asserted their rights under the Copyright, Designs and Patents Act 1988 to be identified as the authors of this work.

British Library in Cataloguing Publication Data
A catalogue record for this book is available from the British Library.

ISBN 0-566-08107-5

Lecture sponsors: Luke Hughes & Company Ltd, Crafts Council, Design Council.

Text designed by David Brown and Bob Vickers and printed in Great Britain by The University Press, Cambridge.

CONTENTS

CONTENTS

FOREWORD

In his first Bauhaus manifesto of 1919 – the one with a woodcut 'cathedral of art and technology' on the cover – the architect and designer Walter Gropius issued a rousing challenge to his colleagues in the art, craft and design worlds: 'architects, sculptors, painters, we must all turn to the crafts'. Translations of this manifesto into the English language almost always make the mistake of turning this phrase into 'we must all return to the crafts'. Not 'turn' but 'return', as if the future of art and technology lay in the past.

Gropius had in mind the craftsperson's understanding of materials, ability to engage in visual research and potential stimulus to industry. These lectures, collected under the title of *On Design and Innovation*, are also variations on the themes of know-how, research and its applications. They range from discussions about the inspirational role of 'the crafts' in industry to case studies of successful design-led companies in both manufacturing and services; from the history of ideas about doing science to accounts of how individual *and* collective efforts can lead to applications of scientific research in the technological sphere. Marshall Meek's now classic Royal Designers for Industry Annual Address on marine design, and in particular on the relationship between cargo ships and the containers they carry, sheds fascinating new light on the old 'form and function' and 'fitness for purpose' debates.

Research, innovation and application, and the importance of investment right along the creative chain: not a 'return' but a 'turn', and a very important one at that; as these lectures show, if ever there was a time to stop mistranslating, it is now.

Professor Christopher Frayling

Rector, Royal College of Art

INTRODUCTION

The issues of converting creativity, invention and innovation into wealth creation are going to be increasingly important if Britain is to compete successfully in the global market. The RSA has a long history of encouraging enterprise. Indeed, William Shipley, a drawing master from Northampton, founded the Society in 1754 'to embolden enterprise, to enlarge science, to refine art, to improve our manufactures and to extend our commerce'. The RSA lecture programme is designed to further these aims and develop debate on these themes.

This book contains a selection of RSA lectures, printed here in edited versions, which observe different aspects of enterprise and industry from the two angles of craft and design and science and innovation. It includes lectures by experts on the crafts, by leading designers with long experience of working with industry, by successful younger designers and entrepreneurs running new businesses and by established scientists and thinkers.

The book begins with two lectures exploring the relationships between the crafts and industry. In his lecture, Sir Nicholas Goodison, chairman of the Crafts Council, calls for more government action to help small businesses and expresses his concern that consumers too often seem satisfied with second rate goods and therefore discourage manufacturers from taking risks in improving the quality of their products. He begins his lecture with a quote from William Shipley which illustrates how the crafts were once perceived and how even the term 'craft' was once so closely associated with industry. Now it has become divorced from it and tends to describe individual craftspeople making unique, individually crafted pieces. The reality is different: craftspeople can work very successfully with industry and now is the time to encourage better links between the two. The question of quality is important and British manufacturers will not succeed abroad if they do not produce high quality goods.

Continuing this theme, the Paul Reilly Memorial Lecture by Robin Levien of the ceramic design consultancy Queensberry Hunt Levien explores the gulf that still exists between the crafts and manufacturing industry and explains how craftspeople can add the special, magical element that can make mass-produced objects stand out from their competitors and appeal more to customers. Craft-based designers have much to offer industry and in order to retain their competitive edge British manufacturers are going to have to embrace this. Both Sir Nicholas Goodison and Robin Levien call for better visual and design education.

The next three lectures are by founders of three small design companies: Helen David of Helen David English Eccentrics, Steve Baker of Tomato and Paul Priestman of Priestman Goode. These are personal accounts of how they set up and now run their businesses, and how from small beginnings their very different companies have become successful and thriving international enterprises. They all agree that sound business planning and management need not limit creativity and innovation.

Helen David tells the story of how her company, English Eccentrics, developed from selling her hand-printed fabric designs at London's Camden Lock and Kensington Market in the early 1980s to receiving her first orders from the United States, and then taking on a business partner and developing a luxury brand.

Steve Baker, managing director of Tomato, stresses the importance of being multidisciplinary in his field of new media. 'Creatives' need to be able to think creatively across the board, from film-making to furniture design, and it is old-fashioned to apply labels such as 'graphic designer' or 'illustrator' to creative people. He explains how, by providing the right environment, a company can ensure that creativity and innovation can flourish. There are two particular challenges for a company such as Tomato: finding a bank manager who understands the nature and potential of the business, and protecting ideas, when only their execution, not the ideas themselves, can be protected by copyright.

In his lecture the product designer Paul Priestman examines the success of his company. From winning an RSA Student Design Award (SDA) in the 1980s for new product development whilst at the Central School of Art and Design, and later an SDA bursary for healthcare equipment whilst at the Royal College of Art, Paul has become known for his innovative radiators, fans and other domestic products, and, more recently, for the tamagochi babysitter. He believes that by working closely with the manufacturers, designers can keep control of their products. To prove the point Priestman Goode has now moved into manufacturing itself with its own production company.

The naval architect and Master of the Faculty of Royal Designers for Industry, Marshall Meek, has seen a revolution in cargo carrying. He describes in his lecture the many challenges that have demanded radical changes in ship design. Credited for the invention of the container ship in the 1960s, he explains how new designs sometimes had to cater for live cargo, such as sheep and cattle, as well as passengers. New ships allowed for containers of cargo to be loaded into cells within the ships, avoiding time-consuming loading and unloading of individual items. Marshall Meek calls the 1990s the 'decade of safety' and comments on improvements in the design of Ro-Ro ships which, until the 1990s, had a basic safety flaw.

The three final lectures, from the Cantor series, look at innovation and inventiveness from an analytical and scientific point of view. They shed light on the so-called 'declinism' in British science, inventiveness and wealth creation. Answering the question,

'Innovation and invention, or insight and investment: what is important?' Sir Alec Broers, Vice Chancellor of Cambridge University, argues that innovation today is no longer the preserve of the individual. Although the individual may still have the ideas, he or she needs the infrastructure, technology and environment, and often the input of colleagues, with which to take them further. It is all about access. He illustrates his argument with various examples of key innovations and advances in electronics, computing and communications, from magnetic recording in the 1900s, to the development of transistors, loudspeakers and magnetic disk memory in the 1940s and 1950s, to Dolby's more recent noise reduction systems.

Sir Robert May, Chief Scientific Adviser to the UK Government, believes that British inventiveness is not in question. British science is a success story. We have an excellent record of scientific discoveries and inventions and our academic research is first class, winning many science prizes, but we often fail to see the connection between discovery, invention and wealth creation. He questions the concept of national competitiveness and also argues that access to high quality scientific and technical knowledge is critical wherever in the world this may be. The lecture describes programmes and initiatives that are encouraging business and science to work together for the benefit of both companies and universities. Research Councils are exploring how intellectual property generated by scientific institutes can be better exploited and how different kinds of collaborative links can be established, but firms must be encouraged to innovate and they must acquire the skills that enable them to profit from technological developments. The UK may be a world leader in producing ideas, but we often fail to exploit this fully and get the goods to market.

The last lecture, by Dr Simon Schaffer, Reader in History and Philosophy of Science at Cambridge University, places the notion of scientific declinism in context with references to Charles Babbage, the nineteenth-century mathematics professor and inventor of the original calculating machine. After exploring concepts of inventive genius and scientific seclusion, he offers an imaginative cure for this 'flourishing of declinism' in suggesting another kind of access – that of access to the general public to dispel myths about science. Integration with society – a moral and social engagement with science – is crucial for its success, and cloistered seclusion is not 'the last best hope of pure knowledge'.

The book covers a wide range of views, experiences and topics, but they are all linked in that they celebrate the UK's rich tradition of invention and innovation and urge us to identify and challenge those obstacles that seem to prevent us from exploiting all this talent.

The RSA would like to thank the lecturers and sponsors who supported the RSA 1997/98 lecture programme on which this book is based.

CRAFTS AND THEIR INDUSTRIAL FUTURE

SIR NICHOLAS GOODISON

Chairman, Crafts Council
Deputy Chairman, Lloyds TSB Group and
Deputy Chairman, British Steel

William Shipley, the founder of the Royal Society of Arts, said that the purpose of the Society was:

> to produce among the boys ingenious mechanics such as carvers, joiners, upholsterers, cabinet-makers, coach-makers and coach painters, weavers, curious workers in all sorts of metals, smiths, makers of toys, engravers, sculptors, chasers, calico-printers

and among girls

> ingenious milliners, mantua makers, embroiderers, pattern drawers, fan painters and good workwomen in many other sorts of business where fancy and variety are required.[1]

The Society's roots thus lie in what we today call 'crafts'. The crafts were perceived to be integral to the industrial processes of the eighteenth century, and remained so for at least a hundred years.

The role of crafts today

That is not the perception today, for two reasons. First, the term 'craft' is less used in industry than it was. Craftspeople are less visible in the modern industrial workplace. A visitor to a modern steel plant or car assembly plant sees and hears very little evidence of the individual workmanship that used to be called 'craft', although it is worth noting that only in the late 1990s has the practice of building and sculpting car bodies in clay been gradually abandoned in favour of the computer, and that Honda has abandoned the use of robots for upholstery and gone back to more traditional methods.

Second, the word 'craft' has been positively encouraged to escape from the manufactory and to take on a specialized meaning of handcraft, as a direct antithesis to the industrial process implied by the word 'manufacture' (as if manufacture did not also mean handcraft). The seeds of this wilful distinction lie within the work of late nineteenth century writers such as John Ruskin, who compared the happiness of the medieval stone carver with the miserable life of the contemporary factory worker, and William Morris, whose views have often been inter-preted as anti-industrial.

Morris, it has been said, did more damage than anybody else to Britain's hopes of industrial success by preaching a return to handmade artefacts. In truth his attitude was equivocal. In her excellent essay on the crafts and industrial design in the catalogue to the exhibition William Morris Revisited (1996), Jennifer Harris made the point that

> not all the designers associated with the arts and crafts movement were opposed to the use of machines. The improvement of commercial design, which had been a cause for government concern since the 1830s, always remained as serious a goal as the restoration of craftsmanship, and William Morris was one of many who recognised that commercial co-operation was necessary for the greater accessibility of their products.[2]

It was, however, the anti-industry side of Morris that took root in the UK. In Scandinavia, where the Morris tradition is also strong, designer-craftspeople and industry have fed off each other far more beneficially.

Bernard Leach was a more recent and an influential anti-industry voice. In *A Potter's Book* published in 1940, Leach said that the potter

> is by force of circumstances an artist-craftsman, working for the most part alone or with a few assistants. Factories have practically driven folk-art out of England; it survives only in out of the way corners even in Europe, and the artist-craftsman, since the day of William Morris, has been the chief means of defence against the materialism of industry and its insensibility to beauty.[3]

The quality argument

Leach went on to say that the work of the industrial potter or potter-artist belongs to a quite different aesthetic category from industrialized manufacture and that the products of power-driven machines 'can never possess the same intimate qualities' as objects produced by the craftsman, even though he conceded that industrially produced objects can achieve an excellence of design.[4]

Lucky Jim in 1954 echoed Leach's view when preparing his lecture on Merrie England: 'Each of us can resolve to do something, every day, to resist the application of manufactured standards, to protect against ugly articles of furniture and table-ware ...'. He was not, of course, sincere, as readers of Kingsley Amis's novel will recall, and spoke some very different words at the conclusion of the lecture when very much the worse for drink.[5]

Bernard Leach's grandson, John Leach, has also preferred the process of personal making – 'there is a spiritual richness which, if I am honest, is more than a little self indulgent ... the trouble with production runs is that in my view they lose the personality of the maker; I have no control over how my designs are made'.[6] He echoes a common feeling among craftspeople earlier in the twentieth century that machines stifle self-expression.

These examples represent only a few of a vast body of writings since the nineteenth century which have sought to differentiate craft, defined as handcraft, from the industrial process. Some of the writers have undoubtedly been swayed by romantic notions of a return to a pre-industrial age, but others, it is only fair to say, were led to their views by the poor quality goods which they perceived emerging from industrial processes. The 'crafts' became a hallmark of superior quality.

The moral dimension

One of the sadnesses of the whole discussion is that a debate about process was loaded with moral overtones. Those involved in the Arts and Crafts Movement shared a belief in the so-called 'honest' use of materials and in the regeneration of people through handwork. From 'honesty' it is a small step to morality. Oliver Watson, the Keeper of Ceramics and Glass at the Victoria & Albert Museum, has written about the Leachian ethical pot. The individual potter working in Leach's tradition was thought to be on the true path, and the collector who bought the pot was purchasing an improved morality.[7] But can a hand-made pot represent an improved morality? Surely not. The truth surely is that the hand-thrown or hand-coiled pot differs from the industrially produced pot because, and only because, it is produced by a different process. They are two different kinds of object. We might well respond more readily with our chequebooks to the subtle differences of workmanship displayed by the one rather than to the greater exactitude of the other. Equally we must concede that we are likely to pay more for that subtlety.

Differences and similarities

To return to the theme of the differences between what we now call 'crafts' and industry, what is 'craftsmanship'? And what do we mean by 'the industrial process'? Nobody has improved on David Pye's modern definition of the word 'craftsmanship' which he published in *Nature and the Art of Workmanship* in 1968. He suggested that it was

> workmanship using any kind of technique or apparatus in which the quality of the result is not predetermined but depends on the judgement, dexterity and care which the maker exercises as he works. The essential idea is that the quality of the result is continually at risk during the process of making.

He called it 'the workmanship of risk'. His definition of the industrial process was 'the workmanship of certainty' which is in its purest state in full automation. Workmanship is exactly predetermined before an object is made.[8]

Crucially, what is common to both production methods is the process of design. What should also be common to both production methods is quality, not just of design but also of materials and finish. It is with these two features, design and quality, that some British industries have a long way to go and could derive much advantage if they could re-harness the creativity of craftsmen and craftswomen. I see no reason why, despite the cultural rift of the last hundred years, craft skills and manufacturing processes should stand at two poles and not again come together.

Crafts and mechanization

Now is a good time to press for the reinstatement of craft at the centre of the industrial process. The crafts are in good shape. As Marina Vaizey has said, 'quality and imagination are the hallmarks' of the crafts in Britain today.[9] We can be proud of our national achievement. Craftspeople are producing work of innovative design and fine quality. Most of them are, not surprisingly, making objects which David Pye would have categorized as the workmanship of risk, in other words one-off items to be bought by individual consumers. But some are using batch production methods and some are having their objects partly or wholly made for them, a point I will return to later. Very few are today alarmed at the thought of using up-to-date machinery to help them in their craft. Craftspeople today are not Luddites. They are using labour-saving machines and computer-aided design.

It is one of the myths created by the anti-industrial culture that such modern aids to manufacture are anathema to true crafts-people. The myth, I have to admit, has been helped on its way by some of them. Edward Barnsley for example, the notable furniture designer and maker, was well known for his refusal to have machinery in his workshop. But even Barnsley relented. Alan Peters, who was apprenticed to Barnsley, completed his time, went off to set up his own workshop and installed a power planer. Barnsley called on him one day and within three months he had bought a power planer himself.

In truth craftspeople have used machine processes whenever it has suited them, and drawing the line between a craft workshop and a small industrial enterprise has never been easy. In the eighteenth century modest industrial enterprises grew from such craft skills as clock and watch making, gold and silver and other metal working, furniture, ceramics and textiles, to mention only a few. Some of these enterprises, such as Matthew Boulton's metal-working factory in Birmingham, a wonder of the industrial world at the time, Wedgwood's ceramics factory at Etruria and Gillows' furniture-making workshops in Lancaster and London, became substantial businesses. They all developed with the use of machinery, but they continued to depend on the knowledge and experience of crafts-people. Batch production became common and in the best cases there was no loss of superior quality.

The development continued in the nineteenth century. Even William Morris did not object to the use of machines, as long as the quality was not reduced. Jennifer Harris, has pointed out that all of 'the contract manufacturers who produced Morris' designs for woven fabrics used the most technologically advanced, power-driven Jacquard looms in their factories'. She also observed that

A. H. Mackmurdo, the founder of the Century Guild Designers' Collective in 1882 'recognised the conflicts in Morris' philosophy and saw an alliance with sympathetic manufacturers as the means of spreading good design practice and educating the consumer'. She reminded us that Christopher Dresser, a contemporary of William Morris and a strong promoter of aesthetic theory alongside the Arts and Crafts movement, was very willing to 'design for the latest production techniques of his manufacturer patrons. His studio was a design practice in the modern sense'. She also mentioned many other examples of crafts-inspired design being applied to batch production of, for example, ceramics, textiles and furniture at the end of the nineteenth century and the establishment of the Design and Industries Association in 1915 (whose members included artists, architects, craftsmen and manufacturers), which aimed to raise the standards in British industry through a restructuring of the relationship of craft and machinery.[10]

Adjustable easy chair and leg rest by David Colwell.
(Photo: David Colwell/Crafts Council)

Working across the spectrum

The crafts today represent a spectrum of making activity. At one end there are those craftspeople working alone making one-off objects; then there are those who batch produce; those who subcontract part of the work, and those who become small industries in their own right. Finally, there are those who use their crafts knowledge to design for industry. More often than not craftspeople work across several of these sectors. Even the potter Lucie Rie made domestic ware as well as unique pieces, and tried her hand as a designer for industry. Sadly Wedgwood never produced her tea set.

Examples of craftspeople's work across this spectrum include, for example, Michael Rowe, who teaches at the Royal College of Art. He is a maker of unique pieces, a metalworker who works in non-precious metals. His works are in effect table sculptures with a series of surfaces playing against each other. They are beautifully considered, meticulously finished and have great presence.

David Colwell (see previous page) is a furniture designer and maker who has ecological concerns to the fore. He uses uses steam-bending in several of his pieces as well as often making use of thinnings which would otherwise be discarded. He is happy to work to commission but batch produces most of his work. His easy chair, one of which is in the Victoria & Albert Museum, and his cafe chair and table, in the Museum of London, have been made for a long time and no doubt now number many hundreds. And yet Colwell has had a problem getting furniture manufacturers to take them up, particularly in this country, and having failed to get the results he wanted has now expanded his own production facilities.

Marianne Forrest, mostly a maker of one-off watches and clocks, has also had her watches made successfully by industry using unique patination methods. A German and a Swiss company spotted her work at the Frankfurt Gift Fair and the association has been fruitful to both sides.

Perhaps the best known knitter in the UK, Kaffe Fasset exhorts fellow knitters to turn away from strict reliance on pattern books and use their colour sense. Companies like Ehrmann have used his designs very successfully in kits and his books have sold in thousands.

The cutler, David Mellor, partly by inclination and partly through force of circumstances has become a part of industry. In the beginning he made all his cutlery designs up himself although he also designed many objects for others. His traffic lights, for example, are still seen everywhere. Later, several of the cutlery designs were made in Korea, but more recently Mellor has brought them back to his own factory near Sheffield.

Wrist watch by Marianne Forrest. (Photo: Marianne Forrest/ Crafts Council)

Robert Welch, a silversmith, is known best for his designs for Old Hall Tableware and for later cast iron cookware made by the Lauffer Corporation in the USA. He still produces his individual work to commission, and said in his book *Hand and Machine* about his own work: 'I believe that is is possible to blend the best of these two worlds, the old and the new, the unique and the multiple, hand and machine, to the mutual advantage of each other.' [11]

Janice Tchalenko is an interesting example of someone who has worked across the spectrum. She makes one-off pieces and has had exhibitions in London and America. She designs for Dart Pottery, a small pottery where domestic ware is made on the wheel and is decorated by hand. She has also designed for Next (see page 34) and was asked to set up a pottery in the Chinese Republic. Another example, Alex Beleschenko (see page 17), is a designer and maker of glass for architecture and has been co-operating with the building industry and architects since the early 1980s.

The economic context

We should encourage more fusing of the craft and industrial processes. As these illustrations, deliberately chosen from a wide field, show, there is no lack of willingness on the part of crafts-people. They are no longer refugees from capitalism. Many are extremely interested in the potential of industry and we should do everything we can to encourage them and use their talent.

Industrially it is a good time to do this. The entrepreneurial spirit is alive and well, a welcome change from the state-dominated period of post-war reconstruction. British industry and commerce are today more competitive, more innovative, more likely to attract bright people as employees and better managed, thanks to the pressures of international competition, the economic and fiscal reforms carried out in the 1980s and the huge advances of technology. Inward investment has flourished, leading to much greater prosperity in areas such as Wales and Scotland and even, against all predictions, to Britain emerging as one of the largest car manufacturers in Europe. Productivity has greatly increased and in many industries it now matches our chief European competitors. On top of all this the service economy has flourished and Britain remains at the top of the league in the export of services, and particularly financial services. There is also a thriving capital market including a sizeable venture capital market helped by tax incentives to those who risk their savings in smaller ventures.

The overall improvement of economic management is not unique to the United Kingdom. Governments throughout the world have come to understand that inflation is intolerable, that irresponsible fiscal policy does not any longer attract votes, and that excessive state intervention in industry leads to inefficiency. The World Trade Organisation has made substantial progress in the lowering of barriers to international competition. Even tax has

Alex Beleschenko: detail of the slender glass tower on Reading Station.
(Photo: Alex Beleschenko/Crafts Council)

become an internationally competitive issue. All this is very welcome and, although there will be short-term upsets, the general outlook for stability and for world trade is better than we have known it since the Second World War.

In the United Kingdom the Government's greatest responsibilities are to keep control of inflation, to reduce barriers to competitiveness and to keep tax rates competitive so that industry can succeed within the framework of responsible monetary policy and competition. There is every sign that both main political parties in this country intend to pursue such policies, as they should if they are interested in long-term economic success rather than short-term political advantage.

Prospects for smaller companies

Much of our economy depends on the success of smaller and medium-sized companies - known as small and medium enterprises (SMEs). According to The Federation of Small Businesses over 90 per cent of UK businesses employ no more than 9 people, but together account for 50 per cent of the private sector workforce. Seventy-eight per cent have annual sales of less than £100,000 and 97 per cent have sales of less than £1 million per annum. Small businesses account for nearly 40 per cent of UK output.

With the reforms of the last 15 years and with the attitude of governments today, prospects for smaller companies are better than they have been for a very long time. Some of these companies have gained because they have become competitive suppliers to large enterprises, including companies established here by Japanese, German and North American owners, all honed on international competition, who have demanded high standards from component and other suppliers.

Other smaller companies make products for the consumer and have been responding to the greater demands for quality, led by the greater consciousness of consumer products in the media and elsewhere. These smaller enterprises make an enormous contribution to the United Kingdom economy and the craft economy is very much part of it.

Improving design quality

It is, however, a very competitive world, and British manufacturers will not succeed overseas, or build a successful home market on which to found a successful export business, unless they produce goods of quality. It is surely in this that Britain most needs to improve performance and particularly in the field of consumer goods. The understanding of customers' needs implies good design. The satisfaction of customers implies good quality of materials and finish. We do not stand much of a chance of competing with producers in low cost countries, such as those in the Far East who pay lower wages, if we do not produce goods of superior quality. Customers won't return for a second bite.

In the High Street it is all too apparent that in a whole range of consumer products we have been overtaken by other countries, partly because of their low wages, but also simply through the comparative quality of design in furniture, lighting, ceramics, glassware and so on. The sadness is that not enough managers in industry in this country have grasped the opportunities. Why is it for example that Italy has a near monopoly on stylish lighting and such a lead over us in well-designed seating? I can see no obvious reasons why we should not be up there leading the world in quality consumer goods. As more manufacturers come to understand the need to produce objects of quality, that's where we could be.

Bernard Leach has something to say about this:

> if the bulk of the pottery turned out in England today [he is talking in 1940, but his words are still relevant] is mass produced and of inferior form and decoration, its inferiority is not so much due to the manner of its production but for various extrinsic reasons, chief of which is the failure of the manufacturer to interest himself in good design.[12]

He ascribed the 'want of artistic initiative on the part of the manu-facturers to the general lowering of taste under conditions of competitive industrialism'.

Leach's point about the general lowering of taste is a good one. There is no doubt that in the past many manufacturers have paid too little attention to design and quality because they cost money, and there has been a market for inferior goods. Alas, there still is, but this is not the way forward. Today competition demands quality, prompt delivery and superior service. A supplier cannot rely in the long term on customers who have bought the second rate.

The value of craft skills for industry
Craftspeople have a deep experience of design and an intimate knowledge of materials and techniques. The application of this experience and knowledge to the making of objects – to the making of better objects, which is what design is all about – can only benefit the producer. There is no better time to encourage a closer relation-ship than now, when the crafts in Britain are flowering so richly, and the quality of the work being produced by British craftspeople is admired so widely. The application of craftspeople's skills in design and in the knowledge of materials, processes and technology can help the production of quality goods enormously.

This is a view championed by several others, such as Mike Press, the Professor of Design and Research at Sheffield Hallam University, who has made the point well.

> We think of craftsmanship ordinarily as the ability to manip-ulate skilfully the tools and materials of craft or trade. But true craftsmanship is much more than this. The really essential element in it is not manual skill and dexterity, but something stored up in the mind of the worker. But beyond this, and above this, it is the knowledge which enables him to under-stand and overcome the constantly arising difficulties that grow out of variations not only in the tools and materials, but in the conditions under which the work must be done.[13]

James Woudhuysen, in his 1996 RSA lecture, observed that 'the crafts may be able to collaborate with big firms both in the customisation of products based on user need, and in the development of product innovations'.[14]

Amongst the practitioners, David Field, the furniture maker and design consultant, speaking at the Crafts Council's seminar 'Furniture: The Challenge of Industry' in March 1997, has criticized the teaching of the making of individualistic furniture as a blind alley. He made the point that craftspeople should be aiming to make money and influence people through industrial production. Luke Hughes, who has made a great success of designing high quality furniture for batch production, makes the point that there are 'few designers working in a factory drawing office who can draw and make prototypes as quickly or imaginatively as a designer-craftsman'.[15] He himself worked as a craftsman making individual pieces of furniture for private clients, illustrating my point that craftspeople have the skills to develop successfully into designing for manufacture by others:

> Designer-craftsmen can now outsource to a factory their own specifications, control their own sales and even operate as a research and development service to a factory that requires their skills. Additionally, they can and should concentrate on keeping their operation locally based. The recognition of each others' [designer-craftsmen and manufacturer] strengths and weaknesses is the basis for forming strategic alliances.[16]

Crossing the divide

It is in furniture that 'industry' practice and 'craft' practice come closest, for very little furniture is mass produced. Virtually all is batch made and most craft furniture makers produce in batches, too, albeit smaller ones. It is therefore easier to cross the divide and many craftspeople have done so.

In a small way the Crafts Council has tried to do something about this in the field of silversmithing. The demise of this trade in which the UK was traditionally a world leader is a sad story. Clearly changes in behavioural patterns reflected in lower demand from the customer have brought about many closures. However, the Council believes that the failure to offer contemporary designs has contributed to the problem. Any trade sector which steadfastly continues to offer only Georgian and Victorian reproduction will not last long and the UK silver trade has paid the price.

In its initiative the Council held a competition for silver objects for the home which could retail at affordable prices. The silversmiths remained responsible for the quality of design and execution throughout the whole process but were encouraged to use various specialist manufacturers for some parts of the finished objects. The whole collection was shown under the title 'Living Silver' in a number of international venues. Steady sales have resulted and the links built up will continue. Several of the silversmiths involved have been taken up by the John Lewis Partnership.

There have, however, been snags in this process:

- There is not enough interest among retailers in commissioning and in stocking high quality consumer goods. Terence Conran has built a business on doing exactly that. His success could be replicated and more work should be sourced in this country.

- Few UK manufacturers appear willing to take the risks inherent in producing new designs. Something is going wrong when a German company runs a competition for students on the silversmithing and jewellery course at Edinburgh and then puts the winners' designs into production, as has happened for several years now. There is a similar opportunity at the Royal College of Art, where David Watkins puts his students through a 'design for batch production' project, but no manufacturer has snapped up this chance.

- British consumers seem willing all too often to put up with the second rate. For this I blame the parlous state of visual arts education.

- Craftspeople should be encouraged to develop their businesses if they feel so inclined and release themselves from having to design, make, promote and sell everything themselves. They may need to outsource some components or invest in more machinery which may be digitally controlled.

- Perhaps craftspeople should offer their design skills, knowledge and expertise of materials to manufacturers. Some craftspeople believe that manufacturers are not interested in their work; certainly some manufacturers are still deeply suspicious of the potential costs of producing quality and are themselves poorly educated in the visual arts. Luke Hughes believes that 'industry's caution in involving those trained in the decorative arts has more to do with the individual's lack of intimate knowledge of relevant technology and its processes and less with a reluctance to pursue new ideas'.[17]

Priorities for action

What are the other practical ways of achieving some advance in crafts input into industry? Government policy is one key area. There will be no successes unless Government continues to provide the overall economic framework within which business can flourish – low inflation, prudent fiscal policies, competition, competitive taxes and so on. Government should also do whatever it can to reduce the red tape to which small businesses are subjected. Michael Heseltine made a much publicized start on this but the European Community through DGXXIII is also attempting to do the same.

Second, there is a huge job to be done in the field of education at all levels, education to improve people's appreciation of the visual arts, in the techniques of craft design and manufacture, education in the techniques and skills necessary in business. None of us can be impressed by the quality of education in the visual arts generally available in secondary schools. Too many people come out of secondary school with hardly any training in the visual arts and with little appreciation of good design, whether it is in architecture, streetscape, art or craft. This lack of visual arts education is at the root of much of our failure to produce, appreciate and buy objects of quality.

In schools, too, there is a need to endorse the importance of learning by making things in both Art, and Design and Technology. Because of the pressure on the curriculum pupils are frustrated when there is no time to develop the practical skills needed for the completion of projects. There is also some evidence that teachers themselves lack the skills of making.

In further and higher education we must look again at the content, structure and funding required to develop work of excellence in studio- and workshop-based courses and also to forge links with industry.

In 1996 the Royal Society of Arts Student Design Awards could not make an award for furniture. The RSA report *UK Design Education: Signs of Strain* points to issues of staffing and resources in higher education and to weakness of basic skills in drawing, presentation and research. However, a few design courses do have links to industry. For example, Cordwainers College has linked elements of its footwear design and production courses with the Royal College of Art and developed a resource base for students and shoe manufacturers in London. Shoe manufacturers can use the college's computer-aided design facilities alongside the students. If students are to build up their knowledge of relevant technology and processes this must surely be one of the routes.

Third, we need to find ways of persuading manufacturers that there is money to be made out of links with experienced designer-craftspeople, pointing perhaps to the evidence of the almost £2 million sales achieved at the Chelsea Crafts Fair and the growing number of examples of craftspeople with these links. The hat makers, Bailey & Tomlin, still make their one-off creations but now also supply all the major department stores in London. In fashion textiles Georgina von Etzdorf started in a small way printing fabric but has built up to a shop in Piccadilly and an international clientele. Emma Bridgewater with her sponge-decorated ceramics finally bought the factory with which she had been co-operating. There are other examples, too.

Fourth, there is room perhaps for more formal links between Chambers of Commerce, representing smaller and medium-sized enterprises, and retailers and craftspeople, so that fruitful ideas can be mutually developed in the fields of design and production. Informal links are just as valuable and should also be encouraged. Information is the key. It is surprisingly difficult for small businesses to source particular materials in the quantity they want, or to find specialist manufacturers for a particular component or process. Who will weave short samples, for example, or who will produce knife blanks (that was David Mellor's problem)? Another way of achieving greater familiarity would be for manufacturers to offer craftspeople short-term secondments, particularly in project research and design. Indeed this is something the RSA's student Design awards seek to set up.

Fifth, I would like to see more research carried out by the Department of Trade into the craft-based industries. The Department produced a useful survey of the furniture manufacturing industry in 1995 which underlined much of what I have said here. It is a very fragmented industry: most producers are fairly small businesses; but it is an important industry to this country. It is largely concentrated on the home market, but it has failed to exploit the market for furniture as 'an important fashion or status statement'. In other words, there is a market for quality which the furniture industry is neglecting; the skills inherent in the craft have not yet been fully exploited. The same can be true of glass, ceramics, textiles, metal working and other trades, and further research would be helpful to point ways to a future of better quality. This is something the Crafts Council could well undertake if it could find the funding to do so.

It is surprising how little research has been done and how few statistics there are on the value to the national economy of Craft and Design courses. The Crafts Council is involved in a two-year research project. Camberwell College and the London Institute are carrying out related research as are the University of Central England and West Surrey Institute. These pieces of research should produce some solid evidence as to how the creative industries are fuelled.

Lastly, there is much further work to be done on the more active marketing of quality. It is no use producing objects of quality if the general public are not going to buy them. To a large extent this comes back to the poor standards of training in the visual arts in schools and in further and higher education, but more could be done to publicize the advantages of quality outside the field of education.

The Crafts Council has a role to perform in this, as it does in education, but so much more could be done. Government should set an example by commissioning work for their offices from good quality manufacturers instead of buying second rate furniture. The Labour Government has said that it will encourage the commissioning of work, and I hope that this is a habit which will become ingrained and will spread to all its agencies. Architects, too, should integrate craftwork into new and refurbished buildings. Employers' organizations and companies should preach the virtues of quality and also set an example by commissioning imaginative work. Prizes could be given for first rate design – perhaps booby prizes, much publicized, should be given for hideous design and shoddy goods.

References
1   *Gentleman's Magazine*, February 1756 pp. 61–2
2   Harris, J. (1996) 'The Crafts and Industrial Design' in *William Morris Revisited*, p. 40, London: Crafts Council.
3   Leach, B. (1940) *A Potter's Book* p.1, London: Faber & Faber.
4   Ibid p. 2
5   Amis, K. (Penguin edition, 1954) *Lucky Jim*, pp. 204, 227, Harmondsworth: Penguin.
6   Hughes, L. (1994) 'Industrial Evolution', *Crafts Magazine* November/December p. 24.
7   Watson, O. (1990) *British Studio Pottery*, pp. 15–16, Oxford: Phaidon/Christie's Limited.
8   Pye, D. (1968) *Nature and the Art of Workmanship*, pp. 4–5, Cambridge: Cambridge University Press.
9   Vaizey, M. 'The Crafts Renaissance', *Antique Collector* December 1992/January 1993 p. 42.
10   Harris, J. (1996) 'The Crafts and Industrial Design' in *William Morris Revisited*, p. 44–5, London: Crafts Council
11   Welch, R. (1986) *Hand and Machine*, p. 17, Chipping Campden: Robert Welch.
12   Leach, B. (1940) *A Potter's Book,* pp. 3–4, London: Faber & Faber.
13   Press, M. (1997) 'A New Vision in the Making', *Crafts Magazine* July 1997, p. 43.
14   Woodhuysen, J. (1996) 'Small Firms, Big Firms and the Future of the Crafts', *RSA Journal* July, p. 77.
15   Hughes, L. (1994) 'Industrial Evolution', *Crafts Magazine* November/December p. 24.
16   Ibid p. 24.
17   Ibid p. 2.

THE IMPORTANCE OF CRAFT TO DESIGN FOR INDUSTRY

Paul Reilly Memorial Lecture

ROBIN LEVIEN, RDI

Queensberry Hunt Levien

C raft is very important to industry, in particular to the manufacturers of low-tech domestic products, the everyday utilitarian objects that fill our homes, often unobtrusive but mostly essential. Tableware, furniture, glassware, pots and pans, cutlery, kettles, toasters, sanitaryware and so on – the best of these products sensitively combine aesthetics with form and function.

Designers with a highly tuned sensitivity to three-dimensional form and materials, gained through craft, have much to offer these manufacturers. In my own experience over the last 25 years there has been a great divide between the crafts and industry, mostly caused by a lack of knowledge and understanding. I sense that this is changing, and I see design as the key to bridging this gap.

The history of Queensberry Hunt Levien
The design practice that I have been working with since the late 1970s was formed as Queensberry Hunt in 1966 when David Queensberry, Professor of Ceramics at the Royal College of Art (RCA) in London, invited one of his most talented students, Martin Hunt, to join him in a partnership. The Queensberry Hunt

partnership was run from the ceramics department at the college; the professors were encouraged by the rector, Robin Darwin, to maintain a professional career beyond education.

After a degree in ceramics at the Central School of Art and Design (now Central St Martin's) in London, I spent three years on David Queensberry's ceramics course at the RCA, graduating in 1976. My further education was effectively seven years of making ceramics. Within 18 months of graduating I was working part-time with David and Martin. John Horler, who had studied ceramics at Camberwell College of Arts, was also employed. In 1977 the partnership became too big to stay at the RCA and we moved to a studio just north of Hyde Park. John and I became partners and the name became Queensberry Hunt Levien.

We work internationally as designers with manufacturers and retailers in many different product categories, but our core business and reputation is in ceramics. Our roots are in the ethos of the UK's craft-based education system which goes back to the Arts and Crafts Movement and also owes a great debt to the Scandinavian craft-based approach to design which has produced some of the greatest designers of the century – one example being Tapio Wirkkala, who trained as a sculptor and continued to sculpt throughout his career. He was an inspirational and multi-talented man who worked as an artist, a craftsman and an industrial designer.

The nature of craft
What are the differences between craft, design and industry and the people involved? It is only by understanding these differences that positive collaborations can occur and therefore progress be made.

An important element of craft is that it involves making things by hand. Craftspeople want to express themselves through what they make and have control over the process. Mary Le Trobe Bateman, who runs the leading crafts gallery in London – Contemporary Applied Art – uses the definition of a craftsperson as someone working with heart, hand and mind.

There has been a massive growth in crafts activity since the war and our art colleges, now universities, have helped to produce an incredibly diverse and highly creative movement. Craftspeople are supported by, amongst others, the Crafts Council and their work is sold through commissions, auction houses, craft fairs, shops and galleries. According to the *Weekend Guardian* of 10 January 1998 the British crafts market is thriving with a national turnover that has now reached £400 million.

This diversity, which makes the crafts so stimulating, includes makers who might be termed applied artists or designer makers producing work that spans from fine art to a hand-thrown porridge bowl. It is amusing to note that in order to determine what duty should be levied on an artefact US customs officers are instructed 'if you can use it it isn't art'.

One of the many examples of crafts' diversity is provided by Dai Rees, who, shortly after leaving the RCA, where he studied ceramics, applied unsuccessfully for a Crafts Council setting-up grant. He was quoted in a *Crafts* magazine article as saying 'I was £6,000 in debt but I knew I couldn't sell my soul with a production range'. Fortunately he is now enjoying great success with his craft pieces.

Craftspeople usually want to be independent and in control of their own destiny. Craft is about a certain lifestyle and scale of operation, small and increasingly urban. What is common to crafts-people's work is some degree of handmaking and an uncompromising pursuit of quality.

Craft and design
So what is important about the best craftwork to design for industry? The answer is that it challenges and extends what can be achieved with materials and processes in ways unshackled by the constraints of manufacturing. Craft objects of quality and beauty can inspire designers and industrialists, but I don't think that the main importance of craft to design for industry is as direct inspiration for designers.

Design as an academic subject in this country is largely a post-war event. It was started by Robin Darwin at the RCA when he became the first rector in 1948. It was, though, categorized in a craft-based way. The departments were called Wood, Metal, Plastics, Furniture, Ceramics, Silversmithing and Jewellery. Darwin believed that the way to train designers was to make them excellent in one area of design and that this would enable them to undertake work in other fields. He also believed that the fine arts influenced design; there was a hierarchy with art at the top.

Design is an ingredient of craft as it is of art or engineering. They are all interconnected and all designers can position themselves somewhere on a line between art and engineering. Design in this context, however, involves manufacturing, whether high or low volume. Whereas a craftsperson usually makes the end product, a designer intends it to be made by someone else. Craftspeople often work on their own; a designer usually has to be part of a team, with the end result being the work of many. A good crafts-person tries to avoid compromise,

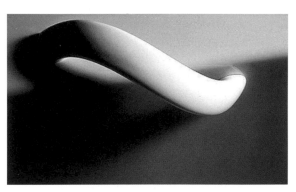

Twisted bath grip for American-Standard combining good looks with function. (Photo: Ivor Innes/ Queensberry Hunt Levien)

while the designer, through the constraints of manufacturing and the marketplace, practises the art of compromise. The designer works with heart, hand, mind and a customer, usually a participating customer.

It is because of these fundamental differences in philosophy and working methods that industry's design problems cannot be solved by trying to reproduce craftspeople's work or indeed by asking craftspeople to independently put forward design solutions. Most craft is actually anti-industry and the better for it.

As a naïve and rather rebellious student at the Central School in 1973 I was preoccupied by these issues. Reacting against the slightly pro-Bernard Leach, anti-industry bias of the course at the time I made slip-cast pots with exaggerated throwing rings and identical transfer prints of an oriental leaf motif. The hole at the top of the pots was also printed so to use them you had to turn them upside down.

The origins of the divide

Distinctions between craft and industry began in the eighteenth century with the division of labour into separate skills. Bernard Leach contributed to further clarifying the distinctions in 1940 when he wrote in *A Potter's Book*,

> The work of the individual potter or potter-artist, who performs all or nearly all the processes of production with his own hands, belongs to one aesthetic category, and the finished result of the operations of industrialised manufacture, or mass production, to another quite different category.[1]

Working with industry

Leach did however suggest that the pottery industry should work with artist-craftsmen. He wrote:

> Every designer either on paper or of model parts should have first-hand experience not only of the processes of manufacture, but also of the limitations no less than the potentialities of his materials. What is obviously needed is a new type of designer who knows both approaches to pottery and can therefore keep industry in touch with fresh artistic expression in the studio. Without such an alliance in the near future between artist-craftsman and factory, it is difficult to conceive how pots could be made in Staffordshire which would be even respectable in the scale of beauty the world has known.

This rather naïve and idealistic approach has been tried on many occasions since the war but there are very few examples of commercially successful collaborations between craftspeople and industry. The potter Michael Cardew tried to remedy this. He was opposed to the idea of producing pots which were only affordable to the rich and went to work at Copeland Pottery in Stoke as a prototype designer without pay. Perhaps the relationship was

Janice Tchalenko design manufactured in Stoke-on-Trent for Next in 1985/86. (Photo: Janice Tchalenko)

doomed to fail. Gordon Hewitt recalls his father, then joint managing director of Copeland, expressing distaste for 'arty farty pots'. In any case Cardew's efforts were in vain. He commented that 'I had been too often invited to admire the smooth, pure white surfaces of fine earthenware and bone china not to know that the potters of Stoke were not about to be converted to something else'.[2] Cardew was ahead of his time as there have since been many examples of highly successful industrial pottery with interesting craft-based glazes, like the current Denby range.

Another potter, Lucie Rie, had discussions with Wedgwood in 1963 and it is widely thought that they should have produced her designs. Paul Reilly, who was Director of the Council of Industrial Design, had introduced Lucie Rie to Sir Arthur Bryan of Wedgwood. Reilly had visited the manufacturer Arabia in Helsinki where he was shown the craftspeople working on the top floor of the factory. He wrote in his autobiography 'Each one had an entirely free hand to produce what he or she wanted in the hope that they would inspire the workers down below, they sought to revitalize machine production through the injection of hand made quality.'[3]

Lucie Rie visited Wedgwood before she did any work for the company and was given a free hand with what materials and style of design she would like to undertake. To Arthur Bryan's surprise she chose blue and white Jasperware from which she handmade beautiful prototype cups and saucers in her own studio. Her designs were never intended to be put into bulk production, so it seems inappropriate that cups and saucers should have been developed. The technique of inlaying white lines, which was one of Rie's studio techniques, requires skill and is slow, so this is a costly way of producing a simple decoration that doesn't really look expensive. It might have been better if she had designed vases and bowls that could have commanded a higher price.

Wedgwood made the mistake of giving Lucie Rie a free hand by asking her to put forward design ideas independently. Successful design for industry is more likely to come from a design brief agreed between designer and manufacturer before work begins.

Hans Coper, who taught me at the RCA and is in my view the most important ceramist of the twentieth century, designed for industry and genuinely welcomed the opportunity to do so, but, wisely, I think, chose to remain a craftsman. There have been more examples of positive case histories in the UK in recent years, such as Brian Asquith's work for Spear & Jackson and Alessi, and Janice Tchalenko's work for Dart Pottery (see page 34), which reflects a trend towards more craftspeople wanting to design for production as well as producing their own craftwork.

Recent research by Karen Yair indicates that it is a craft-based approach to design that is making these collaborations work. The designers understand the materials so they can quickly grasp the manufacturing processes, and speak knowledgeably to everyone involved in the development. The designer with a craft background is better at reconciling technology and aesthetics.

Working with larger manufacturers
With enlightened support from within a company it is relatively easy for craft-based designers who are good, really interested and have the required entrepreneurial skills to work with small and medium-sized companies. But what about big companies who employ thousands of people and have the latest manufacturing equipment to mass produce their products? The design, quality and price of what they make matters a great deal to us – we are all consumers of mass-produced products.

There are big high tech manufacturers of the low tech domestic products that I have described here. Corning Consumer Products Company, for example, besides making the glass ceramic tiles that disperse heat on the space shuttle during re-entry also make glass cookware, such as the Pyroflam range that Queensberry Hunt Levien designed for manufacture in France. They mass produce using the latest high tech equipment. Sales of Corning products amount to around 700 million dollars a year. Eight out of ten homes in the US have Corning products and the average in each is seven items.

Another large manufacturer for whom we have worked for many years is Ideal-Standard, whose turnover in the UK is £85 million. They are part of the American-Standard Corporation who are the single biggest producer of vitreous china sanitaryware in the

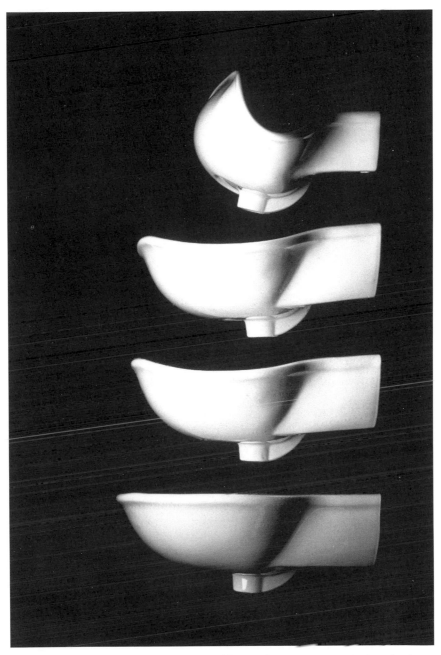

Distorted washbasins — the four mould/design changes required before the basin could be fired without distortion. (Photo: Queensberry Hunt Levien)

world. It was Roger Cooper, the managing director, who had the idea of bringing good design to the fighting end of the market with the Studio range that I designed in the mid-1980s. I have been working with him for over 15 years and his commitment to design has been vital to our success. Designing for large companies involves working with many people from manufacturing, marketing and sales. Without vision and guidance from the top, good design is almost impossible to achieve. There are plenty of good designers but not enough good clients.

We have also designed many ranges of tableware for Thomas which is a division of Rosenthal, now owned by Wedgwood. Rosenthal/Thomas employ 2,000 people and have a turnover of around £120 million a year.

Mass producing craft 'magic'

These companies are large manufacturers but they are producing everyday products from the same basic materials that are used by craftspeople. The culture may be profoundly different but there is much in common. So what is the importance of craft to design for these big businesses?

With few exceptions it is professional designers, whether in-house or as consultants, who have to provide the design solutions for mass production, but for these particular kinds of industries a designer with a partly craft-based education will be better. It is the sensibility gained through making and the values of a craft approach that will enable him or her to humanize mass-produced products. As well as meeting functional needs it is important to get warmth, personality, sensuality into everyday products. These are human characteristics. They are about emotion. When we are confronted by a bewildering choice of products in a shop these characteristics can provide the little bit of magic that makes us choose one product over another.

One endearing human characteristic is that we are not physically perfect, not symmetrical. The artist Andy Goldsworthy wrote in his book *Stone* that when he builds the perfect cairn he will stop building them. There is no such thing as a perfect piece of domestic ceramics. The pursuit of idiosyncratic magic qualities was perhaps what Hans Coper meant when he described himself as being 'somewhat like a demented piano tuner trying to approximate a phantom pitch'.[4] There is a strong parallel here with our approach to design development through modelmaking. We fine tune our shapes through as many iterations as it takes to get them right. Martin Hunt's formidable craft skill enables him to design complex shapes that would be very difficult to draw.

Commercial constraints give us less time than Coper had to refine ideas, so we have to settle for less than ten out of ten. It is interesting to note, however, that most of our contracts with manufacturers are on a royalty basis by which we are paid modest advances with the carrot of sharing in the success later on if our designs sell well. This results in our making the time to indulge in trial and error, evolving our designs through a craft approach. We believe this attention to detail matters to the ultimate success of our designs.

We develop our shapes through both sketch modelling in foam or plaster in the workshop and 3D modelling on a computer. These two processes run in parallel and, unusually nowadays, both are done by the same person. What we learn through sculpting in the workshop we feed into a 3D CAD model. We could design only on the computer and send the digital information down the telephone line, but we believe it is essential to make physical full-size models. It might be a 3D CAD model but during the

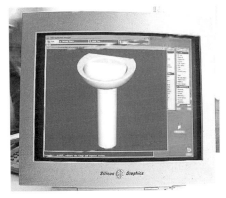

3D CAD model of washbasin built with Pro-Engineer. (Photo: David Sherwin/Queensberry Hunt Levien)

design development stage it is only a 2D image on a flat screen.

For example, we give Ideal-Standard a foam model and a 3D CAD model which they develop further using compatible computer software and computer-controlled milling machines. There is therefore very little interpretation re-quired so the subtleties that we build into our designs stand a greater chance of surviving the development process at the factory. Technology helps us to retain the complex shapes arrived at through hand modelling.

Dave Tilbury of Queensberry Hunt Levien sculpting a washbasin from styrofoam. (Photo: Queensberry Hunt Levien)

Education

This brings me to education, which is so vital to the future of craft, design and industry. There have been some dramatic changes in recent years. When I was a student in ceramics at the Central there were 30 students on the course and the equivalent of five full-time staff. In the department today there are 80 students but still five full-time staff. On some courses students are lucky to get 20 minutes of one-to-one teaching a week. This is resulting in a swing towards teaching theory rather than practice – not good for crafts or design.

There is quite rightly much concern over what happens to students when they graduate, and the numbers certainly concentrate the mind. There are, for example, about 750 ceramics graduates every year in the UK. They are graduating from courses that are primarily about self-expression through craft. A working paper called *A New Vision in the Making* by Alison Cusworth and Mike Press at Sheffield Hallam University, produced in 1996 for the Crafts Council Learning through Making project, revealed that at that time approximately 13,000 full-time craft makers were working in Britain. Of these only 40 per cent had studied on craft courses, of which there were 700. This suggests that at the time of the research each course had only been responsible for approximately seven full-time makers, ever. Quite rightly the paper questions the idea that craft education should have to justify itself purely on the grounds of producing qualified craft makers. Sadly, only 3.8 per cent of the makers surveyed said that designing *per se* was an important element of their working life.

I sense a growing interest in the commercial world amongst the students I encounter and education is adapting to meet this, but there is a long way to go. Role models are important: whether positive or negative, they can help students decide on a direction. Kathryn Lawrence, who runs the ceramics course at Central St Martin's, is teaching her students that commercialism isn't a dirty word. The MA industrial design course at the college is grappling with industrial reality and some of its graduates are finding strategic roles in planning and research as well as design. If you care about the material world and the output of manufacturing industry this is heartening, as the future is in the hands of these graduates.

Our universities are, however, still letting down many of the students on craft-based courses who want to be designers. The education and careers of two young designers, Luke Pearson and Tom Lloyd, who have recently formed the Pearson Lloyd design partnership, demonstrates how things might be improved. The further education of each has combined a furniture course and an industrial design course and both have worked for a year for cabinet makers. After graduating each spent three years working for luminaries of design, Tom with Daniel Weil at Pentagram and Luke with Ross Lovegrove at Studio X. Luke and Tom believe that an understanding of making, process and materials is fundamental to good design, but they offer an industrial design service and are not promoting themselves as craft/designer makers. A fascination with materials and processes and the way the two elements come together is apparent in all their work.

It is the combination of studying on both craft-based and industrial design courses that is interesting. This might seem obvious, but most postgraduate students continue with their degree subject of furniture, ceramics or whatever. When they finally graduate they have a lot of catching up to do if they want to be designers. They often lack the skills required to get that crucial first job in industry or with a design consultancy.

I do not advocate a sausage machine approach to training designers for industry but see the role of education as putting some of the crucial stepping stones in place for the beginning of a whole life of learning. What we need is a new kind of postgraduate course. Karen Yair's research suggests a postgraduate design course that is specifically aimed at students who have completed craft-based degrees. It would have a professional bias and be designed to liberate the inherent skills and values of craft-based designers in a new commercial context. It would combine the further development of the basic skills required by a designer, like using computers, making things and communicating, with the ability to think creatively and to challenge the status quo. The students would be from different disciplines so frontiers would be crossed. It would be a hot house, creative and intellectually challenging. Its graduates would be adaptable and equipped to start a variety of careers in design, manufacturing, marketing, retail, research and beyond. One or two of them may be the enlightened individuals running industry in the future who will give craft-based designers like me a job. As Herbert Read wrote in 1966, 'The sensibility that coursed along the nerves and veins of countless generations of craftsmen must be made to flow again in the veins and nerves of our industrial designers.'[5]

References

1   Leach, B. (1940) *A Potter's Book*, London: Faber & Faber.
2   Clark, G. (1995) *The Potter's Art*, pp. 156–7, London: Phaidon.
3   Reilly, P. (1987) *An Eye on Design*, London: Max Reinhardt.
4   V&A (1969) Hans Coper and Peter Collingwood exhibition catalogue, London: Victoria and Albert Museum.
5   Read, H. (1966) *Art and Industry* (revised edition), London: Faber & Faber.

HELEN DAVID ENGLISH ECCENTRICS – FREEDOM TO INNOVATE WITHIN A STRUCTURED FRAMEWORK

HELEN DAVID

Helen David English Eccentrics

As co-directors of Helen David English Eccentrics (HDEE), Colin David and I run the company together, though each of us contributes different skills. I studied textiles at Camberwell School of Art and went on to postgraduate study of fashion at St Martin's (now Central St Martin's). After leaving St Martin's I taught at various colleges and freelanced, but my designs were considered uncommercial. The directors of one middle-market company for which I designed kept telling me to 'think Wigan'. However, I believed that if people had the opportunity to see my textile designs as made-up garments they would want to buy them. I was also keen to control the design of the fashion item itself along with the textile design, as I believe they go hand in hand.

Setting up a business
In 1982, with £250 inherited from my grandfather, I set up a small print studio on the Thames, working with an ex-student. We hand-printed my designs onto fabrics and then, because we could not afford a baking cabinet to fix the dyes, we used to sneak into a local launderette at midnight and tumble-dry hundreds of metres of fabrics which I pretended were my curtains. Clouds of black smoke

would issue into the night sky as the launderette lady gave me nasty looks. We sewed the clothes ourselves at first – though soon employed seamstresses – and sold them at Camden Lock and Kensington Market. Meanwhile I taught at art schools up and down the country.

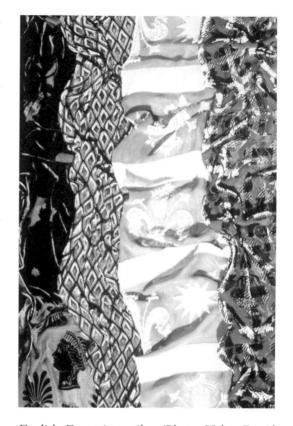

Success in New York

Our label was noticed by the best stores in New York and we began to export. Aware of my weaknesses, I knew it would be safer to avoid dealing with the commercial side of

English Eccentric textiles. (Photo: Helen David English Eccentrics)

the business, so I opted to work with a business partner although it meant selling 50 per cent of my shares. In 1984 I was joined by my first backer and we formed a limited company, English Eccentrics. Orders were coming in from all over the world and in 1985 we had our first runway show.

Managing growth

All this was exciting but we were not a solid company: we were growing quickly but there was no business structure in which we could expand. Production, in particular, was an unresolved area. I was lucky to be supported by family and friends who came to work with me. Colin had been watching the company for some time and felt he could run it in a more structured way. In 1987 he bought out my original backer's shares.

At this stage innovative designs, enthusiasm and energy were the main if not the only assets. The fundamental problem was that the company was growing rapidly without controls or structures. Since 1987 we have tried to turn Helen David English Eccentrics into a professional business while retaining its craft heritage.

While design is the company's core skill, we do not consider it to be sufficient on its own. To compete internationally you have to score highly in every area. We now have departments for all our main areas – design and merchandising, sourcing and purchasing, production and quality control, administration and IT, sales and marketing – with the right people in each department.

Working with the right people

People are the key to our success. We have worked hard at building up the team which is responsible for successfully bringing our designs to the marketplace. Early on we decided to work only with people whom we like and who fit in to our type of organization. They have to be sympathetic with the product and with the rest of the team. As a designer I feel a great responsibility towards our colleagues. We would not keep a stable and happy team if they were worried about job security. The environment is also crucial. Since we moved into a beautiful, light, open-plan building our growth has been strong.

Advantages of planning and structure

With better planning and a proper company structure I feel free as a designer because I am not bogged down by oppressive business concerns, although professionalism and discipline apply to the designer as much as to anyone in a successful company. My role has changed since our early days when I worked in a random, intuitive way. I had no plan by which to structure the designing, no range within which to work and no price specification. That meant I could waste creative energy. Now I create within an agreed long-range plan. I know, for example, what technique needs the longest development time, how many screens I can engrave for printing while keeping the fabric affordable and how much fabric I can use in a garment to meet a price target. However, if I really think that something is so fantastic that it should be carried through, I will make it without worrying about the end price.

Company guidelines

One of the most important things Colin brought to our company was the concept of focus. He achieves this through a series of buzzwords or attributes which provide guidelines for design and for all the other activities within the company:

- luxury – everything we make should both look and feel luxurious;
- glamour – we imagine customers going to Oscar presentations in our evening clothes;
- craft – there is a highly skilled element to our work, which can be embroidered, printed or finished by hand;
- individuality – it is part of my philosophy that the ultimate wearer is an individual, with her own unique history and ideas.

Design, fashion and innovation

The products we make are 100 per cent designer-led, but that does not mean they are uncommercial. We can develop over many seasons a simple tunic that can always be saying something new and yet intrinsically remain the same. Scarves are an important commercial example. When we merchandise our scarf range we have to remember that, as well as complementing our own collection colours, the range must work with what people will buy from other sources that season or may already have in their wardrobes.

Diamond scarves by English Eccentrics.
(Photo: Helen David English Eccentrics)

The other main aspect of our ranges is fashion. This is constantly changing but our customers are not fashion victims. The challenge of the fashion range is that I keep innovating but must not suddenly change direction, as that would lead to customer confusion. If a style is too challenging we might show it as part of a catwalk show and make it only to special order.

I like to be innovative with both cutting and textile design and to keep moving forward. Every season I experiment with at least one new technique. Within the structure that we have created there has to be room for inspiration. In other words, the business structure allows for unstructured design and innovation. The innovation could be a print technique or a design technique using CAD systems, such as, for example, a process that pierces fabric and then seals the edges chemically.

The long-term perspective

We take a long-term view of the business. We learn from our mistakes and try to build solidly. After 10 years we are a reasonable size, with the basic structure in place. We can concentrate on particular areas while everyday business continues. Colin concentrates on developing sales and marketing while I focus on design innovation and promote the company through PR and catwalk shows. We believe that this will lead to future growth. Our long-term aim is to develop a modern, British, luxury brand.

TOMATO – A NEW MODEL FOR CREATIVE ENTERPRISE

STEVE BAKER

Managing Director, Tomato

Tomato is extremely difficult to define in conventional terms. The word design does not fully cover our activities. It is more appropriate, perhaps, to define us by the work we do, which includes television and cinema commercials, print work – from book and museum catalogue design to corporate identity and advertising – product and clothing design, music production, CD-ROM production, and film and television direction and titling. We also set up installations of our own creations. Recently we have published two books of our work, the first of which is already in its second printing, and have had nine international exhibitions. Over the past few years we have been increasingly involved in supplying our own kind of creative thinking for a wide range of clients in such diverse areas as television broadcasting, architecture, museums, cosmetics, car manufacturing and even jewellery retailers.

The origins of Tomato
My background is in recording artist management and I have many years' experience of working with creative artists, exploiting copyrights and negotiating deals. In many ways Tomato is very similar to a group of musicians: they have similar concerns and ambitions and worry about the same type of problems. I have often been motivated by seeing frustrated potential and have for a long time thought that most creative people have extreme difficulty in

exploiting their own talents. Many of them have tremendous problems handling money and sometimes get embarrassed just by having to talk about it. They usually undersell themselves or occasionally go to the opposite extreme, pricing themselves out of the market and become almost impossible to trade with. Seeing talent go unnoticed and unrewarded has always annoyed me and I get great pleasure when work which I played a part in making is appreciated.

Tomato was started in January 1991 by three of us: John Warwicker, my business partner, who is a professional musician, and me. We had met John when he was the art director for A&M Records. He had worked with us designing record sleeves and marketing material and had overseen all our photography and video shoots. He left A&M to be the head of an information design company owned by a film production business which subsequently went into liquidation. We decided to form a new type of company which would act as a vehicle for a number of creative people John had come across in the previous few years who he felt had a similar creative approach and shared the same goals and desires.

We bought an off-the-shelf company whose name was later changed to John Warwicker Limited. John was to supply his creative services, I was to run the business and my partner was to provide the finance which would enable us to buy equipment and finance the cashflow. The shares in the company were divided between the three of us to reflect our relative involvement.

At that time I had a flat in Wandsworth, South London, which we used as the first home for Tomato – for almost six months. The flat was completely open plan, which made some domestic arrangements rather difficult, especially when pressing deadlines resulted in all-night working. Initially most of our clients came from the music industry, where we had strong contacts, and from other previously established relationships such as friends who ran a new advertising agency in Munich.

Next we started looking for a suitable London studio. I wanted to work somewhere like Holland Park, but everyone else wanted to go to Soho. We went to Soho and I'm very glad that we did: the energy and vibrancy of the area coupled with the easy access to excellent facilities makes it hard to imagine Tomato being based anywhere else. Industry was in the depths of recession and D'Arblay Street was covered in 'To Let' signs, so we rented 800 square feet there. Even though we negotiated pretty favourable terms, we couldn't afford to rent the place outright, so we rented one room to a friend and another to my partner as a place to put his growing recording equipment. Various deals were done to make it work.

Surviving in a recession
Starting a business like ours in the middle of the recession was not the wisest thing we could have done. We spent the next 18 months scratching around for work. I took no money from the company for the first two years and my partner received no loan repayments. At one point I had to stop paying John his wages. It was tough.

We persevered, and as the recession started to break and advertising agencies began to perk up we started to get more interesting, better paid work. At that time we also started to be noticed by the press, not just for the work we were producing but also because two of the members of Tomato are in a group called Underworld and they were becoming very well known. Our sleeve designs and videos for the group achieved widespread recognition and the two group members constantly referred to Tomato in their interviews. Our work began to be closely associated with new, edgy music and dance culture. Inevitably that attracted the type of clients that have to sell to the youth market, clients such as Nike, Reebok, Adidas, Coca-Cola and Pepsi.

Controlling growth
An important step was made in August 1994 when we decided to work with two production companies, one here in London, the

other in New York. They have the role of representing us to agencies and clients for the purpose of film and television making. They act as producers for all the work they bring in and add a mark-up on their costs and charge fees. It has been suggested that we could make a lot more money if we had our own in-house producers and this is true – in fact our turnover would be almost ten times larger. However, that would change the nature and balance of the company. The additional overheads and personnel could put us in a position where we had to take on work we didn't want to do just to pay the bills.

Creating space
As activity increased it quickly became obvious that we had to move. I spent almost two years trying to find the right premises. It was an extraordinarily difficult task. We employed agents to look on our behalf and almost drove them round the bend. What we wanted was simple: high ceilings, big windows, lots of light, rough wooden floors, in fact basic warehouse-type space. But we couldn't find it. In order to get something even close to what we needed we considered moving in with our local production company, who were also expanding. We negotiated on several buildings but they all fell through for one reason or another and it became apparent that the two companies' requirements were not really that compatible.

Just when we had got to the point where we couldn't go on any more, a property became available in Lexington Street in Soho. It was 6,000 square feet (about 557 square metres), and had been previously occupied by a post production company that had gone bankrupt. It was dingy, and had been separated into many different editing areas and machine rooms with no natural light. It was far too big, needed months of work, over £100,000 of demolition and renovation and was way out of our price range. So we took it.

Again, many deals have been done to make the property work. We did everything on a shoestring, employed architects that were fresh out of college and had to persuade landlords who had spent their lives covering up floorboards, brick walls and rough ceilings that we wanted to expose them all.

The conducive environment

One of the main reasons that Tomato exists is to provide an environment within which creatives can thrive and produce the work they want to make. A fund is available to finance personal creative work on films, exhibitions or publications. All of the members of Tomato are freelance; they own their own equipment and even their desks and chairs. It is vital to the ethos of the company that all of the members feel free to come and go as they please. All of the jobs we do are taken on because individual creatives are specifically interested in that particular job. No-one is ever given a job to do, no-one ever works on something they don't want to work on.

Quite often there will be more than one creative working on a single project at any one time. In this instance, a group of creatives may get together before a job is confirmed and all express an interest in the project. Normally one person takes on the task of leading the project, and the fees are apportioned according to individual involvement, which sometimes changes during the project so fees splits have to be reapportioned.

Avoiding limiting labels

Another important aspect of Tomato is the refusal to put limiting labels on individuals. In my experience, creative thinkers are capable of applying their abilities to many different areas. All of the creatives of Tomato are multidisciplinary. They can all apply their talents to a wide range of creative areas from film-making to music-making, from furniture design to corporate logos. I'm not sure when the trend started of giving creative people labels such as 'graphic designer' or 'illustrator' or 'director', but I know this particular brand of old thinking is completely inappropriate for Tomato and for most other creative people I know. A label implies a limitation and at Tomato we are limited only by our imagination.

Much of the work produced by Tomato is credited only to Tomato. For example, we published a book, called *process*, where none of the work was credited. Our corporate showreel listing our work has none of the directors' names attached to it. This sublimation of the ego has had many benefits. Our insistence that the work is seen to be a product of a group of people has forced clients to think about the creative process in a different way. We have often had calls demanding to see a particular director's showreel; we respond by saying that there isn't one but we can send a Tomato showreel.

The company structure

We changed the structure of the company again a couple of years ago, formally changing the name to Tomato Limited and making all the creative members into equal shareholders. In our current configuration Tomato acts very much like an agency, negotiating fees, invoicing and chasing for payment, and retaining a percentage before paying through to the individuals concerned. Much of the way that Tomato works is based on trust. There is no need for complicated written agreements between ourselves, and our shareholders agreement, which we have to have by law, includes such phrases as 'enlightened self-interest' and 'love'. This is clearly an unconventional method of doing business and I am often faced with the blank stares of people who just don't get it.

So we have a company which is owned by the freelance creatives whom it represents. It exists in order to promote, protect, enable, nurture and administer its owners – and hopefully to produce beautiful pieces of work. It seems to work, at least for the time being. What I have great difficulty in understanding is why other creative companies don't work in the same way.

Banking

I was asked to talk about some of the challenges we have faced and there are two specific areas that we continue to have problems with.

The first one is banking and the second is to do with copyright and ideas.

It seems to me that the recession caused some permanent changes in the way that the major banks run their business. I find this rather ironic because I believe the banks had a major part in causing and prolonging the recession, but that would be the subject of a much longer, separate discussion. It used to be the case that you could develop a relationship with a bank manager who would visit your premises, get to know you and your track record, understand your business and even make helpful suggestions. You would talk regularly, and if you needed an overdraft or loan, it could be arranged with a single telephone call. This doesn't happen today.

When we moved to our new building I projected that we would need a small facility of maybe £40,000. Bearing in mind that we were by that time turning over more than £1 million per year, had been trading for five years, had never been overdrawn and had virtually doubled our turnover every year since we started, I expected an automatic 'rubber stamp' approval – but nothing of the sort. In fact the hoops that they wanted me to jump through made me wonder why I had bothered to stay with the same bank for more than 15 years, putting several million pounds through various business accounts and making sure that the bank was always kept informed.

Tomato is not designed to make a profit. In fact, if we do make a profit, it shows that we have retained too high a percentage from the creatives. So our balance sheet and profit and loss are not particularly inspiring, but it would not take a rocket scientist to determine that we were doing very well. I find it frustrating that there is so little faith in individuals and track record; I came to the conclusion that it would be much easier to borrow a couple of million and disappear to the South Seas than arrange a measly £40,000 overdraft. In the end I told the bank to forget it and we have financed everything out of cash flow. We've been able to do this only because all my major creditors are also the shareholders of the company.

Copyright and ideas

The second challenge is more difficult and potentially more dangerous to us. It stems from the fact that Tomato is really in the business of selling ideas, whether it's a marketing idea, a communications concept or a complete new look for a media company. Unfortunately, the only way you can sell an idea is to describe it and you can't copyright an idea, only its execution.

There is no way that you can stop an unscrupulous client from taking your ideas and using them without employing you. You have to trust that if the client likes your ideas then they will use you to implement them. This is not always the case and it is particularly galling to see your ideas misappropriated, mutilated and generally abused when all you have been paid for is a pitch.

The paid pitch is a particularly vulnerable position but also difficult to turn down, especially if you know you're going to have to invest a lot of time and money in order to present your ideas. In America, a paid pitch means that copyright of the material produced for the pitch transfers to the client. In fact every time you pitch an idea to a client you face the risk that it will be used without your being reimbursed for it. It's happened to others and it's happened to us; it will undoubtedly happen again.

One good idea can be worth millions to a large multinational and that same one good idea can be taken away from its creators and messed up because the implementation has been bungled by people who misunderstood the depths of the concept behind the idea. The whole subject is fraught with problems and I am not even close to finding a solution. If anyone has a good idea of how to solve it I'd be very interested in hearing from them.

The future

So what does the future hold for Tomato? The only thing we can

be certain of is change, and we embrace that change. We now have
an apartment in New York and we hope to open Tomato New York
in the near future. We have many goals and ambitions which can be
summarized by wanting to 'making a difference' on a global stage.
Ultimately I feel it is worthwhile to attempt to leave this world a
more beautiful place than when we entered it.

PRIESTMAN GOODE – TAKING CREATIVE OPPORTUNITIES

PAUL PRIESTMAN

Priestman Goode

M y consultancy, Priestman Goode, is based just off Marylebone High Street in London. We work for companies all over the world designing a wide range of products and also manage large projects, such as refrigerated cabinets for Marks & Spencer which we worked on from concept right through to installing the cabinets on site. We have also manufactured our own products.

Establishing a consultancy

After studying at the Central School of Art and Design (now Central St Martin's), where I won an RSA Student Design Award bursary, I undertook a postgraduate design course at the Royal College of Art (RCA). One of the products I designed in my last year there was a megaphone which won a Japanese international design competition. The prize money allowed me to set up in business, working from my bedroom. When I went to Japan to collect the prize I made contacts with Japanese manufacturers – my firm is still working with some of them.

At the RCA I designed some hot-water radiators which attracted favourable press comment. A consortium of businessmen put up money to have them made, but there was absolutely no interest from manufacturers. I was so frustrated at having people wanting to buy non-existent products that I manufactured them myself in a garage. An electric convection heater attracted a lot of press coverage, particularly in *The Sunday Times*, which published a feature on 100 people, including me, who they thought were going to be big in the 1990s. Because of that article, an Italian company decided to manufacture the radiators in return for paying a royalty to me. I also obtained a large contract from another company which asked me to design some other products. That was the beginning of becoming a consultant.

Sharing the load

At that stage I took a studio in Chelsea, renting most of it out to help pay for it, and work started to come in. I needed someone to share the load, so formed a partnership with Nigel Goode, a fellow designer who had been at the Central School with me and had worked for some big consultancies. That was in 1989 and it has been a successful partnership. Soon after Nigel joined, we won a contract to redesign the whole Belling range of cookers and appliances. It was a vast project and we were able to employ quite a few people.

The aesthetic element

One of our other products, an electric convection heater, came about from a visit to a factory in Italy. I saw some industrial elements sitting on the floor, took one away with me and was excited about the possibilities of making a heater out of them. They normally run at red-hot temperatures in water but if the power output could be downrated it would be safe enough to touch and could be made into a product. The interesting thing about this is that putting a slight bend into an upright shape gave the heater character – without that the product would be nothing. This is an aspect of design we try to push the whole time: it does not cost any more to make a beautiful product.

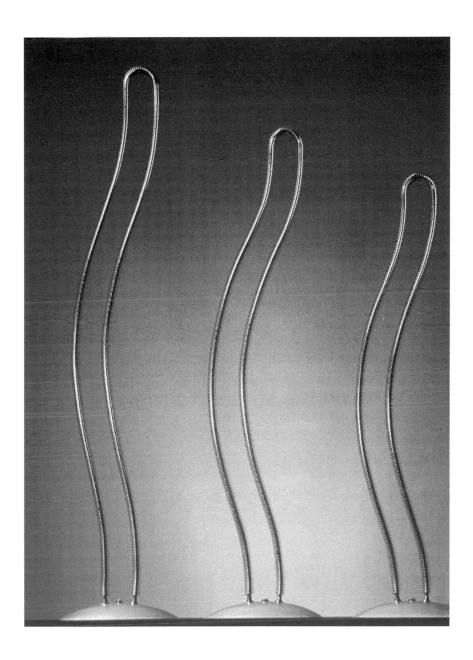

Electric convection cactus heaters, produced by Bisque in Italy.
(Photo: Priestman Goode)

Computer communication and design

A washing machine we designed for a Korean company is an example of the way we, like many other product designers, now work. We do not have drawing boards any more but high-powered computers on which we produce five or six concepts to present to the client, perhaps by video conferencing or e-mail. The customer chooses an image and asks us to develop it. We do so on computer, making a virtual product. It can be revolved and you can even see inside, but it exists only in the computer. When the customer is satisfied we transfer all the information needed to manufacture it. This speeds up the development and manufacturing process. What you see on the computer is what you get in the end.

Concept for an electric fan with all moving parts in soft fabric, making it safe to touch. (Photo: Priestman Goode)

Environmental considerations

A product currently being developed by an American company is a domestic fan. These are usually ugly, bulky things, with most of the product being a grille to stop you touching the blades. I had the idea of making the blades from kite material. The motor spins the fabric and centrifugal force makes it rigid and introduces air into it. It is convenient for a small space and, more seriously, for transport. When products are manufactured in the Far East it is both expensive and costly to the environment to move bulky objects round the planet.

Manufacturing and quality issues

When we redesign products after only a short time some people think it a waste of resources to retool so quickly. Yet manufacture at high volume means machines wear out and have to be replaced. This is a good opportunity for the manufacturer to update and keep ahead of the competition.

Another domestic radiator we designed replaces a towel radiator made out of a series of bars welded together. This is an expensive manufacturing process and uses a lot of energy. I had the idea of feeding a continuous length of tube into a computer-controlled machine which can adjust the way the material is manipulated. It coils and bends the tube, which is then welded at various points to give a rigid structure. That makes a heat-efficient object which is also fun to look at. These radiators now sell all over the world.

When one product is designed for many countries we have to bear their different requirements in mind and sometimes need to allow for small variations in function and design, besides simpler issues such as colour changes. It is be particularly important to get the quality right, as many plastic objects appear cheap.

Minding the electronic baby

One of our recent design projects is the tamagochi babysitter. We read that tamagochis (mini electronic 'pets') were being banned from offices and schools and thought it would be useful to be able to pop it into something that would look after it. We produced computer images and our friends in Cambridge came up with electronics. After a feature in *The Sunday Times*

Tamogochi babysitter. (Photo: Priestman Goode)

we were inundated with enquiries from manufacturers and licensed the tamagochi babysitter to one of them.

Creative collaboration

The future of product design lies in taking it right through from concept to production and keeping control. You achieve successful products through that continuity and from working closely with manufacturers. We are now moving into manufacturing for our clients through our production company Plant Ltd. We have a 'village of specialists', a group of good people with whom we work. This is the modern way: brilliant people coming together to create fantastic products.

They That Go Down to The Sea in Ships – A Revolution in Container Design

Marshall Meek, CBE, RDI, FEng

Naval architect
and
*Master, Faculty of Royal Designers for Industry**

> 'They that go down to the sea in ships, that do
> business in great waters, these see the works of the
> Lord, and his wonders in the deep' Psalm 107, 23–24.

Any little success I have enjoyed as a designer came from being close to the user or operator of my designs. This ensured that effort was not wasted, that the end product was achieved in the shortest possible time, and that it reasonably satisfied the customer requirements.

For me this was easy because as a naval architect I was either employed on the staff of my company, a major shipowner, or contracted to work for other associated ship-owning companies. What I designed was therefore what was required by those companies and it had to meet the strict requirements of the particular service involved, usually within a tight time schedule. We can all quote familiar examples of design failings which we believe we experience almost daily – the television on/off control that is

* This is an edited version of the RDI Annual Address given by the then new Master of the Faculty[1]

invisible, taps you cannot turn with wet hands, and so on – so we all wonder at times whether designers actually use the products or consult the people who do. The result is that sometimes the user has a diminished respect for the designer. Designer and customer, user or operator need to be totally at one.

My origins had little to do with my eventual professional activities: my father was a sculptor in a little country town in mid Scotland. But as I watched my father sketching out and carving on gravestones I was unconsciously learning to appreciate the beauty of lettering and graphic design. As I watched my father operate the modest derrick crane he used to lift the gravestones in our back yard, I was absorbing the principles of mechanics. And when he sharpened his chisels by heating, hammering and tempering them, I was being introduced to the elements of metallurgy. When he erected his work in the local churchyards I gained a knowledge of foundations and brickwork. The fact that he had served with the Royal Engineers throughout World War I no doubt instilled in me a respect for and attraction to engineering. In such ways we all gain from our early environment and surroundings, and my entrance to the world of shipbuilding and design, which was totally fortuitous, benefited from experience that I little regarded at the time.

When I became naval architect for my company, Alfred Holt & Co (later Ocean Steamship), the first ship for which I was totally responsible was a very complicated passenger and cargo liner commissioned for the trade between Fremantle in Western Australia and Singapore. It had, for reasons of economy, to replace two existing ships which were due for scrapping after many years of service. This was in itself a problem because the ports and the berths only allowed a very slight increase in the size. There was no possibility of simply doubling the ship size. The nature of the cargo was unusual, for the ship had to carry an intimate mix of 200 passengers and large numbers of sheep and cattle – sometimes as many as 5,000 sheep. On the southbound journey she carried the passengers and 700 very wild cattle from north-west Australia. There was also general cargo, liquid such as palm oil or latex, and some refrigerated goods. The regular quota of dairy cows destined for breeding by certain wealthy Singaporeans had to be milked *en route* by the Malay seamen. We had to design a small on-board dairy to make use of the products. The sheep were carried in two tiers below deck, but the cattle obviously needed full headroom so the upper sheep platforms were capable of being hoisted to the deckhead.

The feed for all these animals was a problem, as indeed was the ventilation of the sheep and cattle spaces. Out of consideration for the passengers, we carried out extensive wind tunnel tests to make sure effluent and vapours were directed elsewhere, and particularly away from the swimming pool area, hence the large masts which doubled as ventilation ducts.

A final problem was that while the cattle were being loaded at the remote ports of Broome and Derby in north-west Australia the ship had to sit aground on the sea bottom, high and dry for a few hours, because of the extreme tidal conditions in these parts. This highly unusual practice caused two serious complications. The ship had to be specially strengthened to take the bottom; and the period for loading the cattle was strictly limited to one tide. As the animals had seldom seen human beings before, and reacted accordingly, the whole concentrated procedure of loading them tended to be interesting for all on board.

Breaking design tyranny
From the building of that ship there developed a long, fruitful and perhaps rather unique association with the Royal Designer for Industry Neville Ward, which lasted for many years and ran through the building period of a variety of ships. The designer of something as complex as a ship cannot and should not be responsible for every aspect of design. Neville Ward was an interior designer who had a particular feel for ships and an amazing ability to coerce and cajole reluctant or hostile shipbuilders into doing unheard-of things like moving pillars or bulkheads to facilitate the designing of interior

The Centaur, designed to replace two older passenger cargo ships.(Photo: Marshall Meek)

accommodation. For example, he questioned whether the passenger or crew cabins need always have their boundary bulkheads square to the centreline of the ship. This had been standard shipyard practice from the earliest times, but it meant that at the aft end of the ship, where the shape and curvature were pronounced and where the accommodation was sited, each cabin had a progressively less sensible and useable shape. To make these bulkheads square to the outside curve of the ship rather than to the centreline was heresy. It broke what Ward called the 'tyranny of the T-square and set square'; and it turned out to be perfectly feasible, providing rooms of better configuration. M.V. Centaur, as this ship was named, entered service in 1964, the product of a young ship designer who has often thought since then that he would not again be brave enough to tackle such an irreconcilable set of requirements!

Post-war design challenges
The Ocean Steamship Company (familiarly known as the Blue Funnel Line) were masters of the cargo liner trades, mainly running

from the UK to the Far East and Australia. The ships were fast, high class vessels operating to strict bus-like timetables and carrying high value cargo. Naturally the ships were expensive. After the long period of steady replacement of wartime losses, with successive classes of ship little different from each other, my arrival as responsible naval architect coincided with the requirement for larger, faster and more sophisticated vessels. Accommodation had to improve for more demanding seafarers. Not only was ship speed to be increased but there had to be better ventilation for cargo, air conditioning in the cabins, better maintenance procedures, more electronic equipment, faster and more powerful cargo handling gear. All these meant increased cost and higher skill in designing.

The Glenlyon class of the 1960s were now bigger and faster than their predecessors, but they still carried the well-known Blue Funnel company trademark of the tall, straight funnel. It was when the company moved on to the next series of cargo liners, the Priam Class of the late 1960s, that we not only perpetrated the sacrilege of amending the funnel shape, but produced the ultimate in fast, powerful and expensive cargo liners. These were the answer to our competitors who had continually sought to outstrip us in speed and efficiency. They were majestic in appearance and effective in operation, yet they taught me serious lessons.

One was the need to establish the limits or boundary conditions very clearly before a design is committed. The Priams were governed in size, and particularly in width, by the width of a particular dock gate at Birkenhead. It was the secondary entrance to our principal dock on the Mersey. It would have been used in an emergency if the main gate was not operating. In actual fact the eight Priams never used the gate in the end and so carried a penalty in having non-optimum dimensions for the rest of their lives.

Even more importantly, these Priam ships were designed so that the size of the hatchways giving access to the holds, and the shape of the holds themselves, were not suited to the carriage of containers. Containers as a means of carrying cargo were just round the

Ship bar and cafeteria designed by Neville Ward, RDI. (Photos: Marshall Meek)

corner at this time. Ships of this type normally last some 20 years or more, especially if cared for in the way my company cared for them. The fact that six of the eight ships were up to a year late in delivery from British shipyards did not help: containers arrived in service by the late 1960s just as the Priam ships were developing what should have been regular and profitable service. They were just not designed for containers and attempts to stow them either in the holds or on deck were little better than failures. The designs never had a chance to justify their initial high cost, although the accommodation, again by Neville Ward, was generally recognized as superb. Up to that time, the company had never taken out hull insurance on its ships, such was the confidence in their design and operation.

The container revolution
The advent of the container was by far the most important event in my career. It brought a revolution, and it happened because ship owners realized, perhaps belatedly, that ships were vehicles but spent far too long acting as static warehouses. The process of stuffing individual items of cargo into ships' holds and between decks was just too time-consuming. The proportion of earning time spent at sea carrying freight was too small compared to the time spent in port. In addition, the whole business of documenting cargoes in a multitude of small lots was unproductive and unnecessarily complicated. The Ocean Steamship Company was certainly better than most but still achieved only 53 per cent of time at sea with the Glenlyon Class, and 60 per cent with the Priam Class. (The Liverpool Bay class containerships (see page 80) improved the time at sea to 82 per cent.) The Priams owed their improvement to more powerful cargo-loading equipment and better-shaped cargo spaces, so speeding the loading or removing of the cargo. But ships still needed to be stuffed and unstuffed. The containership totally altered ship-operating economics. One containership replaced six or more conventional cargo liners. The reduction in ship numbers had a major effect on people as well as on economics.

The container concept developed rapidly during the mid-1960s and the industry finally opted for containers loaded vertically into cells within the ship and supported internally by cell guides, with a proportion of boxes above deck sited on the hatches. That decision led to the requirement for new berths at the ports and for new, very large portal-type cranes and very large storage areas for containers. The costs were high.

Because no single company could face up to the cost of the new type of ship, the new port facilities and cranes, and not least the thousands of containers, OCL (Overseas Containers Ltd) was formed as a consortium of Ocean, P&O, Furness Withy and Cayzer Irvine. Other international consortia followed.

New design implications
When we were given the task of designing the world's first ocean-going container ships we faced questions no-one had ever faced before. There were many unknowns. How easily would conventional cargoes go into standard size containers? How big a share would the companies acquire of the global trade between these countries? Would it expand? What was the optimum speed of such ships? How big should they be? And, ultimately, how many ships would be needed? The answers had to be found, and quickly, because OCL was determined to lead the world.

As designers, we were close to the arguments and to the decision-making, but there was one particular critical ship design consideration that had never been faced as acutely before. The top deck of the ships was to be almost totally removed to allow containers to be loaded vertically for maximum speed of loading and discharge. This demanded a fundamental reappraisal of the ship structure. Conventionally and from time immemorial ships had bent: they either drooped at the ends, 'hogged'; or they 'sagged' at the middle under the effect of waves. Head or astern seas and waves provided the greatest forces on the hull. The twisting effect of sailing in seas oblique to the direction of travel was quite small.

Now for the first time ships were to twist appreciably in oblique seas as well as bend, because the restraint arising from the top of the hull was effectively removed. The bending and the twisting stresses would be additive. Could ships be built that could withstand the forces and yet provide the clear opening up of the deck area that was necessary?

It was a time of intense activity. Designers could not wait for inspiration. We had to act on the information available on what could be researched quickly. Unfortunately for ship designers it all happened a little before computer-aided design became available and before powerful techniques such as Finite Element Analysis became current practice. We had to depend on personal judgement, calculation and physical model testing. At all times the shipping companies involved were fully understanding of our problems and never at any time hesitated in agreeing expenditure on research and development. They sensibly weighed the cost of any technical

Container ship showing stresses encountered in rough seas. (Photo: Marshall Meek)

proposal against the enormous outlay involved in the overall project, but the designer was close to the user and could get quick answers.

The 'standard' container was internationally agreed in 1966. The basic dimensions, the strength of the box, and particularly of the corners, were fixed. This was vital for determining how high a stack of loaded containers could be. Just as the container dimensions eventually determined the length and breadth of the ship, so the stack height largely determined the depth of the holds. The manufacturing tolerances of the container dimensions were also agreed. The clearance between container and the vertical cell guides within the ship needed to be decided because any heeling over would make free running of the containers in the guides difficult. To this end we built a mock-up of the cell guides in the German shipyard where five of the first six ships were being built. This was tilted to simulate ship movement and a container was lifted and lowered by shipyard crane within it until we were satisfied with the operational clearance between container and guide.

By far the most critical stage was determining the hull structure. Because of the absence of almost the whole top deck, the most vital structural feature became the 'strength box' at the upper corners of the remaining narrow deck and the hull, incorporating the massive steelwork and welding connections that needed so much care in design and manufacture. There were, of course, hatch openings in what remained of the upper deck and the corners of these openings were the most critically stressed areas of all. The smaller the radius, the higher the stresses, and we wanted the corners to be small so that we could fit as many containers in the opening as possible. For such a new structural concept we consulted all available sources and specialists, both corporate and academic.

A novel experiment was carried out on the first container ship of the class as it was loading in Rotterdam for its maiden voyage. The ship was quite literally and deliberately twisted while lying alongside the berth. This was done by filling diagonally opposite water ballast and fuel tanks and by placing heavy weights on deck. The stresses at the hatch corners and elsewhere were measured with strain gauges in order to correlate the calculated stress with actual in-service behaviour. We had to calculate and add to this stress, the forces and loadings on the hull that would come from waves at sea, and also the likely worst asymmetrical loading of containers that might be experienced during service. The unhappy result was that the stress at the hatch corners came out at higher than the yield strength of the steel material. This is normally inadmissible and naturally caused concern.

Until the strength in these areas could be improved some time later (by adding a heavy strength bulwark at the ship side) limitations were placed on the operation of the ships. The ships' masters were given maximum allowable stress readings from a number of stress gauges throughout the ship so that they could decide whether to alter speed or change course if the permissible stress was exceeded. It was at this point that our principal structural design consultant wisely suggested that because we were in such a high stress regime we must now consider fatigue stress and fatigue life of the steel. This was the first time fatigue stress had had to be brought into the picture for ship structure. It had been assumed up to that time that only brittle fracture of hull steel needed to be seriously considered as a source of danger. Fatigue of steel structure generated from the continuous passage through a succession of waves, sometimes exacerbated by whipping motions, has had to be taken very seriously ever since. Its study is an important part of all ship structure design today.

We had to play very safe on every aspect of design on the basis that to get anything wrong, like losing containers overboard, would be deleterious in the extreme to a brand-new concept. The strength of the lashings needed to retain containers above deck was just one major design problem. In calculating this, we assumed maximum rolling motion together with maximum pitching, which since proved to be an over-pessimistic assumption. An intriguing feature of such container ships is that for a given number of containers on board, about one third of the whole cargo can be carried on the deck. In effect this provides a more economic ship since that portion of the cargo above deck does not need ship structure around it.

The first six ships were called the Encounter Bay Class, five built in Germany and one at Fairfields in Govan on the Clyde. In spite of many teething problems, they were regarded as highly successful in spite of being 'first of class'. They have only recently been considered for scrapping, having served well over 30 years.

Maximum speeds and dimensions

Ship speed for the Encounter Bay Class was largely determined by the maximum horsepower from the steam turbines of the time that could be put into a single propeller. For the next series of Far East container ships, however, it was agreed to take everything to the limit, whether size or speed, so that no competitor could beat us. We were tired of what we considered lesser companies trying to upstage us. Having talked closely with the designer of the QEII, which had 120,000 horsepower provided by two engines on two propellers, I felt I could accept something less for what were, after all, cargo ships. So I asked for 100,000 horsepower, again on two propellers, and was somewhat disappointed that the OCL consortium chairmen felt I should be given only 80,000. Such were the lofty decisions taken at the heyday of British shipping. That machinery output was still able to provide speeds as high as the modern aircraft carrier.

As to size, my maximum limit theory held good. At that time and for almost 30 years thereafter it was believed that merchant ships should be able to transit the Panama Canal if any sort of round-the-world service was contemplated. Hence the only limit to the size of our ships was the dimensions of the Panama locks. Only quite recently has the decision been made that larger vessels might indeed be more economic if it can be accepted that they will operate only on one side of Panama or the other, and so we now have what are called Post Panamax Containerships

An interesting point was that while the Panama Authorities of the day declared what the maximum beam and draught of ships should be, they would never give a maximum length. The maximum beam allowed two feet (61 centimetres) clear each side in the locks, to allow for a ship listing to one side or the other. The draught was determined by the amount of rainfall in the area and the level of water in the Gatun lake which filled the lock system. But length was something of a secret and it was presumed that this was because the Authorities wanted, for safety reasons, to keep ships well short of the maximum dimension between the lock gates. The Panama Canal is such an important waterway not only to the US but to the world's trade that there must be no question of damage occurring to the lock gates. Because of the importance of this length dimension to my maximum limit concept, I visited Panama and persuaded the Authority to fix a maximum length – 950 feet (290 metres).

In pushing the size of the ships to the limit we knew we were having to accept dimensions which were not ideal. The Panama locks, completed in 1920, were not designed for modern 1970 container ships. The width is not great enough, proportionate to the length. Hence our ships were accepting too narrow a beam and this had a direct influence on their stability. We had to build-in the capability of filling ballast tanks with sea water during the voyage to compensate for the consumption of fuel oil in order to keep the ship stable. This meant a cost penalty in operation. In addition, very close control had to be kept on the way the containers were loaded ensuring the heavier ones were lower down in the ships. The ships were designed as steam ships with two boilers, with twin turbine machinery and two propellers and they consumed about 400 tons of oil per day when running at maximum speed. Being designed to run direct from Europe to Japan the bunker capacity was large, to say the least.

The Liverpool Bay Class Ships

Although the designing of these much larger ships, the Liverpool Bay Class, followed dangerously close to the entry into service of the first Encounter Bay Class, and indeed overlapped in time, we were able to avoid any further structural design problems even though we had little time to gain in-service data from the first ones. One structural item, however, did cause much design work on the bigger ships. There were to be only two hatches in the width of the ship. This meant that the hatch covers, which are in the form of removable steel lids, were very large in span. They had obviously to carry a full stack of deck containers, yet the weight of the cover itself could not exceed the maximum weight of the maximum – 40-foot (roughly 12-metre) – container. This was because only the shore-based container crane is available for the lifting of both containers and hatch covers, and the crane is designed only for the weight of the 40-foot container, 30 tonnes.

It is not often that the naval architect has to face such a weight limitation. We had to have a serious look at the way civil and aeronautical engineers design their structures before we could satisfy this strict limitation. Because the hatch covers are no more than load-bearing lids to the upper deck openings, they do not contribute to the strength of the hull. There is an appreciable and noticeable movement of the hull relative to the hatch cover when the ship is bending or twisting in a seaway.

The accommodation in all these container ships was again designed by Neville Ward. In the same way that great care had been expended on the structural design, so the interiors received most careful attention. In merchant shipping it is not usual to employ specialists in this area, but such was the determination to have ships of the highest quality in all respects that the extra cost of providing top class accommodation was seen as a necessary part, all the more so as the crews were to spend more time at sea per year.

Five of this Liverpool Bay Class were built, all in Germany. They cost just over £10 million each in 1969, probably equal to between

Liverpool Bay container ship. (Photo: Marshall Meek)

£80 and £90 million today. Such were the inspired decisions that were made when it was almost impossible to calculate or estimate the requirements for a wholly new transportation system; and such was the boldness and conviction of those who determined British shipping policy in those days.

All these ships have proved highly successful and are still in service, but the effect of introducing such ships on the shipping scene as it was before containerization has been profound. The carrying capacity of each ship had increased enormously compared with the earlier cargo liners. The Liverpool Bays of 1972 carried a quantity of cargo over six times greater than that carried by a Priam Class cargo liner of only five years before. Multitudes of cargo liners were rendered obsolete with all the unhappy consequences, not only on seagoing folk, but on all the subsidiary businesses depending on them – the dockworkers, stevedores, ship repair companies, tally clerks, right down to the corner shop and pub. Once the further decision was made that these latest ships would not use the company's traditional home port of Liverpool, that city suffered a blow to its prosperity from which it has never recovered. From that time on, container ships have been entering service in ever increasing numbers in every maritime nation, but apart from those being built in Germany, Denmark and Poland they are built mainly in the Far East.

Designing for hazardous cargo

My next major exercise in ship design was with LNG (Liquid Natural Gas) carriers, still in that exciting period starting in the 1960s and running into the late 1970s when shipping was making tremendous strides forward. However, the two LNG carriers I was involved in were a joint exercise with the shipbuilders Chantiers d'Atlantique of St Nazaire and typified what so often happens with major engineering projects where it is so difficult to identify a single individual designer.

Liquid natural gas carrier Nestor discharging its cargo. (Photo: Marshall Meek)

The liquid gas cargo is carried at a temperature of -160 °C. It is difficult to conceive what this means in practical terms, but the fact is that if any of that innocent-looking clear liquid at that temperature reaches the ship's steel structure, brittle fracture follows immediately and the results can be catastrophic. There are therefore a number of highly effective forms of containment and insulation for protecting the ship steelwork. When the complication of cargo containment is added to all the intricate control and safety measures required to handle such cargo, the result is an extremely expensive ship.

The Ocean Steamship Company owned one of the two LNG ships that we built, the Dutch Nedlloyd company owning the other. Compared with the highly successful container ships, these two gas carriers were an unmitigated disaster. The hoped-for charter which was in the background when the ships were ordered in 1970 never materialized. In spite of enormous efforts to find other sources of employment, I found myself responsible in 1977 for laying up both of them in Loch Striven in the Clyde estuary. There they lay until relatively recently, having been long since written off by the companies. None of us blamed our company directors for the decision to build the ships. We were all party to it and shared the enthusiasm for reaching out into new ventures, especially those of us who enjoyed new technology concepts.

The influence of cost factors

The 1970s were a time when the greatest efforts went into ship design for fuel economy. The colossal rises in oil price in 1973 and 1979 meant a total reappraisal of design, the most striking result being that the optimum design speed for ships decreased. This was a total contradiction to the trend that had existed through all my previous experience when each successive ship was faster than the previous one. It was surprisingly and quite painfully difficult for the naval architect to accept this phenomenon. Many studies had to be made into improving the engines (which were by now mainly diesel), the hull form and the propeller. As a result, at the end of the decade the average ship was using only one half of the fuel that was being consumed 10 years earlier, though the speed of the ship was less.

The decade of the 1980s saw strenuous efforts to reduce the number of people on board. Having taken a grip on fuel cost, companies found that the manning costs were the next significant area for treatment. With new systems and new equipment, with work study and with automation, very large reductions in manpower were achieved. Over my period of involvement the complement of the average merchant ship today is about one third of what it was in the 1950s.

The decade of safety

At one time I thought the 1990s would see some further major change in the way sea transportation was organized. I envisaged some new methods of consolidating cargo into still larger units with some new ship types appearing. I was wrong. The 1990s can be called the decade of ship safety. The loss of the Herald of Free Enterprise off Zeebrugge in 1988 was a landmark event and it was followed by the Estonia disaster. They were both Ro-Ro (roll-on, roll-off) ships. As long ago as 1976 I had stated my view at a conference on Ro-Ro ships that a basic vulnerability existed. My team of naval architects and I were convinced that the modern ferry, scontinually increasing in size, with its large open deck so near to the waterline, offended basic naval architectural principles. These principles imply the containing of any water entering a ship, and the modern Ro-Ro ships had no way of doing this. I have been involved in the discussions about making them safer ever since, always having the hope that stricter rules would be applied. It is good to be able to record now that improved survivability is required by international regulation, but it has taken a long time to reach this point. Increased safety always costs money.

One of the most frustrating studies has been into the loss of MV

Derbyshire which occurred in 1980. In spite of intense study and the holding of a six week Formal Inquiry we do not yet know why this quite modern well-manned and well-maintained British ship was lost with all 44 lives on board. It is a matter of great satisfaction that the wreckage was found in the Pacific Ocean in 1996. There has been a further underwater examination of the wreck but this may still not yield a definite answer. At least the maritime industries will have caught up a little on the aircraft investigators who have been more successful in the past in finding and even retrieving aircraft from the sea.

There were less publicized losses over these years, particularly in bulk carriers, where a steady stream of problems is only now being arrested. There has been a growing awareness amongst the public concerning safety in general, and in the maritime world we have had to devote a great deal of effort to designing safer ships to satisfy this public concern. The process continues.

The future of cargo ships

At the end of the decade I am seeing the fulfilment of my vision of a new consolidation of cargo movement, in the form of the very large post Panamax Containership. Once the constraints of the Panama Canal are removed the field is wide open again and not unnaturally the search is on for the optimum size. The Liverpool Bays had a maximum capacity of about 3,000 TEU (Twenty-foot Equivalent Units – the equivalent of 3,000 20-foot [roughly 6-metre] containers). Current new designs have increased to 5,500 TEU. Most of them are being built in the Far East with only Denmark and Germany having any other presence, and there is now talk of building even more capacious vessels.

My design career has covered a period of very great changes in marine design. New ship types have proliferated, showing that specializing in one trade with a strictly limited type of cargo is more economic than building ships to cover a range of business. It is the increase in size of ship over my 50 years of involvement that is the most noticeable feature. The reasons for this are: the very real economies of scale that apply to marine transportation; better design techniques; more understanding of and better data on sea states and therefore more precise knowledge of loads and forces on the ships; and computer-aided design. During those 50 years we have seen a change away from the overriding importance to the seafarer of preserving the ship and its cargo from the sea. Because of the changing nature of the cargoes carried and the greater concern for the marine environment we now have to attach as much importance to preserving the sea from the ships' cargo.

It is still an unfortunate fact that ship designers, however close they are to the ship operator, still have difficulty in going to sea, and experiencing what actually happens there. This is a serious problem and should be overcome through a greater willingness of ship owners to take designers to sea, and a greater desire on the part of the designer to go. Only in this way can the designer claim to be really close to the user and operator in his real environment.

The pity is that most of the activities described here, whether in shipbuilding or in ship operation, have been lost by Britain. The company I worked for at one time owned 120 ships. Today they have none. The same can be said of most other major UK shipping companies who were contemporary with us. I hope that present and future government administrations will view the nation's marine activities in a more favourable light and encourage them instead of discouraging them, as has happened over the last 20 years.

Note
1   The distinction Royal Designer for Industry (RDI) was established by the RSA in 1936 to enhance the status of designers in industry and to encourage a high standard of industrial design. Up to 100 designers can hold the distinction at any one time. The RSA also confers the title of Honorary Designer for Industry (HonRDI) upon those who, while not citizens of the UK, have rendered signal service to industrial design.

Innovation and Invention, or Insight and Investment: What is Important?

Professor Sir Alec Broers, FRS, FEng
Vice Chancellor, the University of Cambridge

In this lecture I briefly trace the evolution of some key advances in electronics, computing and communications and discuss the factors that characterized their development. I then gather in a table my conclusions about these factors together with those for several other advances not described here. From the table I conclude that the key advances in these fields, as the title of this suggests, have depended more on insight – defined as in-depth understanding of the fundamentals of the technology – and on a serious commitment backed up by adequate investment, than they have on flashes of inspiration and invention. Furthermore, almost all of the fundamental advances have been brought to reality in the research laboratories of large organizations, either those of large industrial companies or laboratories supported by governments. I include university research in the large organization category because it is generally funded by government or large industry. It is rare that advances come out of small enterprises; many highly successful companies have naturally grown from small beginnings but usually by taking advantage of fundamental advances made in the laboratories of large organizations. General factors not included in my Table 1 – because they apply universally – are the need for insight and the need to exchange people between research, development and manufacturing organizations to ensure the rapid and effective transfer of this insight.

In many fields of science and technology we are in an era where the ideas of a single person seldom lead to significant progress. The ideas of individuals, and of course all ideas originate with individuals, must fit into a matrix of innovation before significant progress is made. The innovation matrix extends across groups of researchers and in many cases across nations and the world. If a researcher is not a part of the worldwide technology network, they are unlikely to succeed.

The genius of minds combined

This is the area of greatest change in the last 100 years. It was possible for the physicist J.J. Thomson to make fundamental progress in the discovery of the electron using relatively simple equipment with only a handful of co-workers. Similarly, De Forest and Langmuir developed the vacuum valve in small, relatively isolated groups. However, since then developments have involved progressively larger teams working with the support of large concerns.

A typical example of this was the development of the transistor at AT&T's Bell Telephone Laboratories in the 1940s by the group led by Bardeen, Brattain and Schockley. Its creation was not an isolated stroke of inventive genius but the outcome of a focused project to develop a solid-state amplifier to replace the vacuum valve, the result of the coordinated genius of top minds. Today, the scale has increased further and the development of a new microelectronic chip, today's equivalent of the vacuum valve, will take the combined genius of hundreds of researchers.

Another characteristic of the present environment is the high rate of change. Few high technology products last more than a few years: for example, Hewlett Packard reported in their 1996 annual report that only a fifth of the products they shipped in 1996 were more than three years old. This incredible pace of development makes it essential to set aggressive schedules and, through adequate investment, ensure they are met. It is pointless shipping out-of-date appliances or equipment. There is no sign of this pace slackening, particularly as the underlying driving force of relentless improvement and reduction of costs continues.

Origins of technologies

MAGNETIC RECORDING

Magnetic recording was first demonstrated by the physicist Vlademar Poulsen in 1900 using iron wire. Plastic recording tape coated with iron oxide was developed in Germany during the First World War. Its use for recording data for accounting purposes was first investigated by James Bryce in 1937 and at IBM in 1953 he built the first computer tape memory systems. Since 1953 immense improvements in density and speed have been made through improved magnetic materials and by reducing the recording head gap and the distance between the recording head and the tape. These advances continue today.

Thus, whilst the concept for magnetic recording came from an individual, practicable recording was realized through the German government's drive; one of the massive injections wartime gives to technologies. It then took a large company to support the research that made it possible to build a practicable memory for a computer.

MAGNETIC CORE MEMORY

Magnetic tape recording was valuable for storing large quantities of data but access to specific data was slow. The desire to shorten access time gave the impetus to develop the magnetic core memory where data was stored in tiny iron oxide cores. The cores were arranged in a two-dimensional array and threaded with the wires through which current was passed to switch and read their magnetization.

Ideas for using ferromagnetic rings to store information were proposed in the mid-1940s. The most advanced work was by An Wang, a PhD student at Harvard, in 1949. Munro K. Haynes, a student at the University of Illinois, improved on Wang's work by showing that the number of wires passing through the cores could be reduced to two if Deltamax cores were used. Haynes joined IBM and with others produced the first operating core arrays in May 1952. The first large-scale core memory was incorporated in the SAGE prototype computer delivered to MIT in January 1955. This consisted of over 13,000 cores knitted together with hair-thin wires.

The evolution of core technology, while it shared some of the underlying physics of magnetic tape recording, was different. The technology emerged in university research and was then brought to fruition by a large company.

Magnetic disk memory

The most remarkable magnetic memory is the disk memory: magnetic material is spread onto the surface of a small disk like a gramophone record and information is then written and read with magnetic recording heads that 'fly' less than a ten-thousandth of a centimetre above its surface. The analogy of a 747 plane that is flying a centimetre off the ground is often used.

The disk memory concept was first explored at the National Bureau of Standards in Washington by Jacob Rabinow in 1950. The first successful writing and reading from a multidisk recorder was demonstrated by IBM in February 1954 and they delivered the RAMAC (Random Access Memory Accounting Machine) disk file in June 1956.

Dramatic progress on disk drives has since been made, through improvements in magnetic media and by reducing the recording head gap and the gap between the head and the disk. Heads are now made using chip fabrication methods and this has allowed multiple heads and closely spaced tracks to be realized. This technology originated in a government laboratory and was brought to practicable realization by a large company.

ELECTRONICS

Electronics is of importance to all the technological developments of the later twentieth century. The intelligence that is provided by complex electronics extends and expands human intelligence and thereby finds ubiquitous application across human endeavour.

THE ELECTRON

Electronics began with the discovery of the electron by J.J. Thomson at the end of the nineteenth century. Thomson was working with glow discharges that occur between metal electrodes in a glass 'bottle' form which most of the air has been removed. He found that the glow extended through a hole in the positive electrode and fluoresced where it struck the glass. This had been observed by a number of physicists. His genius was to deduce that the fluorescence was caused by a stream of particles, electrons or 'corpuscles' as he called them These carried an electric current and it was known that if electric currents were rapidly varied, electromagnetic waves were produced and in a complementary way the waves would induce currents.

These waves were to form the basis for radio and television, but before those revolutionary advances could be realized means were needed to amplify the weak currents induced by the waves. The vacuum valve created by De Forest provided this amplification. De Forest found that the current flowing between the electrodes in a vacuum tube could be controlled with a metal mesh, or grid, placed between the electrodes. A small negative voltage and almost negligible current produced a much larger change in the current flowing in the tube. He had invented the triode vacuum valve.

The vacuum valve was subsequently improved by a succession of individuals, but it was the massive development effort deployed in the world wars that brought it to the point that it could be mass-produced for domestic use, first for radios and then for televisions. The valve emerged from the initiative of individuals who built upon fundamental scientific investigations. Government and then industrial support on a large scale made it practicable for general consumer use.

THE TRANSISTOR

The transistor was developed in a different way. It was the outcome of a project involving a team of physicists at Bell Laboratories specifically assigned the task of developing a solid-state replacement for the valve. They were using semiconductors, materials which had been explored in Britain during the Second World War in connection with radar. An electron current can be controlled in a semiconductor in a way which is impossible in metal.

THE MICROELECTRONIC CHIP

The development of the valve, at least in the earliest stage, was accomplished by a series of individuals. The transistor needed a small team supported by a large organization. The next device, the integrated circuit chip, needed an even larger effort. Again the original ideas were those of individuals but almost immediately relatively large teams became involved because there were so many techniques to be perfected before it could be ensured that every device on the chip worked.

Building 200 billion transistors into a chip involves research teams of hundreds. The individual ideas of these engineers are essential but only in the context of the overall project. The scale of the effort can be understood by examining one part of the fabrication process – lithography. This is the process used to etch the electronic components into the silicon slice. The aim is to achieve further miniaturization, because smaller transistors are faster, cheaper and consume less power. It is generally agreed that these benefits will continue at least until dimensions reach a twentieth of a micrometre, that is, five to ten times smaller than they are today.

However, a twentieth of a micrometre is beyond the resolution of ultraviolet (UV) light protection cameras used to print the images for these circuits. An alternative will have to be found, but the task is not solely one of resolution, it also concerns economics. It has been possible for 30 years to use electron beams to write a hundredth of a micrometre patterns – at a high cost. It is clear that we can make devices beyond this resolution limit, just as we have been able to make aircraft that fly faster than the speed of sound, but only at a cost that is too high for mass production. It is almost one thousand times more expensive to print images with electrons than with light.

More than twenty alternatives to optical lithography are being investigated. To gain resolution, they use shorter wavelength radiation than UV light, either extended ultraviolet (EUV), electrons, ions or X-rays. The ideas and insight of a large number of engineers are needed to explore these alternatives and make the crucial decision as to which one to use.

Lithography represents only one third of the overall fabrication process and fabrication is only one factor in the development of new chips. The design of the devices and circuits, and the overall architecture design of the chip have to be considered. Engineers and scientists covering fields as disparate as circuit theory, polymer chemistry, solid-state physics and pure mathematics must work in a closely integrated manner. This cannot be accomplished with a small organization.

AUDIO SYSTEMS

Audio systems involve different technologies. Marked improvements have been made in the clarity of high fidelity sound over recent decades, most of them due to advances in recording techniques and in loudspeakers. Amplifiers have been essentially perfect since the late 1950s. Advances in recording, including the long-playing record, the compact disc and, more recently, digital tapes and discs, have been made in the laboratories of large companies.

LOUDSPEAKERS

Advances in loudspeakers, however, have been made in relatively small companies, many of them British. This has been a field where art has been mixed with science and it has been possible for relatively small groups to make significant advances. In particular, appreciation of the sensitivity of the ear to phase in determining sound location led to speakers in which the driver units were vertically aligned rather than randomly placed in the enclosures. These speakers produce a clearer stereo image. As the general requirements of high quality have become widely known, however, the emphasis on low cost efficient manufacturing have increased and the ability of small companies to survive may be in question. Nonetheless, relatively small companies remain successful and have been able to sustain their own research effort. This is an exception to the other cases I describe.

DOLBY NOISE REDUCTION

Dolby noise reduction is an example where the genius of one person, Ray Dolby, using a relatively small organization, succeeded in the arena of mass-produced consumer goods. Dolby applied the concept of the compander, a device that reduces unwanted background noise when selecting a desired signal, to reduce background hiss in magnetic tape recording. The concept of the compander had been used in experimental science, Dolby himself using it to enhance the signal to noise ratio in electron beam microanalysis, so the idea could be said to have had its origins in university research. Dolby combined electronic circuit innovations with an understanding of the characteristics of the human ear to use the compander to produce the original system for the audio tape.

Dolby's basic approach has now been extended to the more complicated theatre and domestic surround-sound system. In fact the technology is now so complex that relatively large teams of electronic, software and behavioural scientists and engineers are needed. Again the ability of an individual to make a significant contribution is diminished. Dolby Laboratories can no longer be considered a small organization.

Classification of technologies

Table 1 identifies the factors that were important in the development of a variety of technologies. The second column indicates whether advances have been made in an evolutionary manner through problem-solving. The third column shows where new materials have been important. The fourth and fifth columns show whether the advances have been made by applying existing concepts or by employing new concepts or inventions. The final column shows where the technologies were conceived and developed.

Technology	Factors involved in development					
	Insight relying on fundamental understanding	Evolution through problem-solving	New or improved materials	New application of old concept	New concept	Source Industry/ Academic large/small
Magnetic tape memory	✔	✔	✔		✔	Indiv + LI
Magnetic disk memory	✔	✔	✔	✔		LI + govt
Magnetic core memory	✔	✔	✔		✔	Univ + LI
Transistor	✔	✔	✔		✔	LI
Integrated circuit	✔	✔	✔	?	?	LI
Single transistor memory	✔	✔	✔	✔		LI
Miniaturization						
Optical lithography	✔	✔	✔	✔	?	MI + LI
X-ray lithography	✔	✔	✔			Univ + SI
E-beam lithography	✔	✔	✔	✔	?	Univ + MI/LI
Dolby sound reduction	✔	✔		✔		Indiv + SI
Modern loudspeakers	✔	✔	✔		?	SI/MI
Walkman	✔			✔		LI
Digital TV	✔	✔		✔		LI
High Definition TV	✔	✔		✔		LI
BBC microcomputer	✔	✔		✔		Univ + govt + SI
IBM personal computer	✔	✔		✔		LI
Apple Macintosh	✔	✔		✔		MI/LI
Optical fibres	✔	✔	✔		✔	LI
Global positioning system	✔	✔		✔		govt + LI + SI

LI - large industry   MI - medium-sized industry   SI - small industry   indiv - individual   govt - government   univ - university

Table 1 Classification of innovations

The white heat of change

Technology is advancing at a pace considered impossible only a decade ago and success in most fields of complex modern technology depends on large teams of scientists and engineers working in close collaboration. The Wright brothers may have been able to work alone and one could say that Frank Whittle's first experiments with the jet engine were also made with a small group, but those days are gone. Large teams of collaborating engineers and large, high risk investments are essential to pull off the high value-added projects of today, such as the building of cars, ships, communication networks, electronic chips and computers.

Almost all advances are made in an evolutionary manner by solving problems at technology frontiers. Quantum leaps forward and revolutionary concepts are the exception, and more sophisticated science and innovation is frequently required to implement an invention than was involved in the invention itself. New materials are frequently the driving force for significant advancement.

There is no universal way to innovate, but it is clear that for innovation to flourish, enterprises of all sizes should be present and should collaborate; large enterprises working with small and medium-sized enterprises, and universities collaborating with everyone. A significant number of the advances made by large companies fall outside their business interests, and spin-offs and start-ups are effective in capturing the commercial potential of these ideas. It is difficult for small companies to work on base technology: they are better off collaborating with larger organizations.

ARE WE GETTING BETTER AT EXPLOITING OUR SCIENTIFIC AND INNOVATIVE CAPABILITY?

SIR ROBERT MAY, FRS

Chief Scientific Adviser, UK Government
and
Head, Office of Science and Technology

There is no doubt that British science is a success story. With 1 per cent of the world's population we carry out 5.5 per cent of its research. We have an excellent record of scientific discoveries and inventions – the laser, radar and the Worldwide Web to name a few. Our academic research is world class and its quality is demonstrated by the attraction it holds for researchers from all over the world. Our record of achievement in major science prizes is second only to the USA, and the best in the world (at both the start and finish of the twentieth century) when expressed per capita.

However, we should not be complacent. Although in many fields the UK is already a world leader in producing innovative ideas, we have not always been as good at fully exploiting this potential advantage for ourselves. For example, one of the anomalies in the UK's economic performance is that despite access to a world-class science and engineering base, productivity growth in the past has been poorer compared to our major competitors in all but a few industries. Figure 1 demonstrates this point.

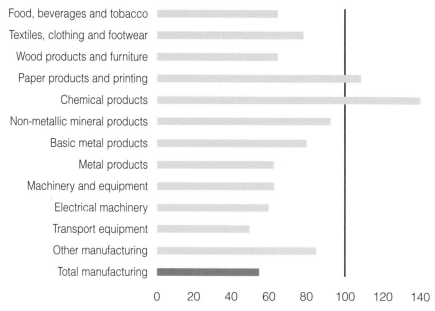

Note: Productivity measured by value added per hour worked. Rest of G7 excludes Italy.

Figure 1 Productivity in UK manufacturing relative to the rest of G7 countries in 1993 (G7 = 100). (Source: Pilat)

I shall look firstly at the contribution of science and technology to economic and social advance; secondly at recent efforts to improve our performance in exploiting new science and technology; and thirdly at how successful these efforts have been. Finally, I will suggest the approaches we might take in the future. Much of the data that I will draw upon has a manufacturing slant, but this is not intended to understate the importance of the service sector.

The economic contribution of science
We can all think of inventions and scientific advances that have led to improvements in the quality of life: vaccines and antibiotics are just two examples out of many. But the contribution of science is

more profound than simply the sum of individual inventions. Its impact is felt in the quality of life people experience and in changes to our society and culture.

At the turn of the century half or more of the workforce was employed in agriculture and fisheries. Today the proportion is around 1 or 2 per cent, who produce more food. Advances in medical science lead us to expect a more healthy life which lasts longer than that expected by our grandparents and great-grandparents. At a more routine level, a holiday abroad was unheard of for the majority of the population one hundred years ago, yet most people now travel abroad once a year for a well-earned break.

Underpinning all these changes are advances in basic science, which is one of the UK's major strengths. The quality and excellence of the UK science base is well recognized by the international community. It is a major force in research with an 8 per cent share of the world's scientific publications and a 9.1 per cent share of world citations. In relation to money spent on basic research in science (including medicine and engineering), the UK has, throughout the 1990s, published more papers than any other country, Sweden, Denmark and Switzerland lie close behind. By these admittedly iffy measures, the UK is markedly the most cost-effective producer of basic research among the G7 countries.

Intuition tells us that science is a major contributor to competitiveness and economic growth in the long term. However, the nature of scientific research and its exploitation means that it is difficult to measure precisely or predict its economic contribution. Early work by Schumpeter[1] on the nature of technological processes led to the widely accepted theory that the long-term performance of an economy depends on its ability to exploit successfully new technological possibilities. More recent work supports this theory and in particular that a country's GDP (Gross Domestic Product) and growth in productivity are considerably enhanced by increases in technological activity and a strong scientific research base. A recent US study attributed half that country's growth in productivity in the twentieth century to the fruits of new knowledge (the other half to more familiar increases in labour and capital).[2]

In the longer term the economy can only grow if it finds ways to produce more outputs for less inputs or develops a more valuable range of products. The economy must be able to innovate, which means that it depends on the abilities of its people to think of new, better ways of doing things or develop new insights into science, engineering and the whole range of studies that underpin business success. Thus a country's access to high quality scientific and technical knowledge is a necessary condition for economic prosperity. It is not, however, a sufficient condition. In order to exploit this knowledge there need to be the right incentives for universities and companies to exploit their research assets and for companies to have the right assets, including a willingness to take risks, to absorb the knowledge and turn it into profitable output. The Government needs to promote these increased connections between the innovative science and technology base and the market place.

In 1995 a report by the Science Policy Research Unit[3], commissioned by the Treasury, on the relationship between publicly funded basic research and economic performance also concluded that such research seemed to have a substantial impact on productivity. However, the work also found that the use of basic research as a source of new information is not the only economic benefit and that there are a number of other benefits arising from such research. The first of these is that basic researchers tend to create new instrumentation and methodologies. For example, a chemist – let us call her Jane – invents a new widget to use in her R&D that when applied to a production process elsewhere in the company cuts costs. Secondly, the skills developed by those engaged in basic research yield economic benefits when individuals move from basic research. So when our chemist Jane moves from R&D into marketing she takes her problem-solving skills with her. Thirdly, basic researchers gain access to networks of experts and information.

So when Jane has to market a product in Japan she is able to ask her scientific contacts in Japan for advice. Fourthly, those trained in basic research tend to be particularly good at solving complex technical problems. Lastly, there are also economic benefits from the creation of spin-off companies.

In my job as Chief Scientific Adviser I see two essential tasks: preserving our scientific excellence and doing a better job of exploiting its potential in the UK in order to enhance the quality of life, wealth creation and the competitiveness of our businesses. Many areas of manufacturing do not have a good record of translating scientific excellence into industrial success. Figure 2 shows the relative R&D performance of UK sectors compared to the group of the five major industrial countries (G5 – US, Japan, France, Germany and UK). A figure of one hundred, for example in food,

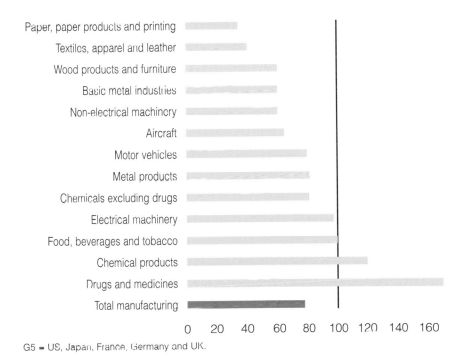

G5 = US, Japan, France, Germany and UK.

Figure 2 R&D intensity in UK manufacturing 1994 (relative to G5 average = 100). (Source: R&D Statistics)

beverages and tobacco sector, shows that it is spending as much on R&D, as a proportion of 'value added' as its foreign counterparts. A figure greater than one hundred, for example for chemical products, shows that the sector spends more on R&D as a proportion of value added than its foreign counterparts. With the exception of the pharmaceutical, chemical and petrochemical sectors, UK industry's R&D investment record is relatively poor and manufacturers do not appear to be as committed as their foreign competitors to spending on innovation.

The Government's contribution

Analysts and commentators also point to other weaknesses in UK companies which hold back their ability to exploit successfully new knowledge or new technologies. These weaknesses include the education and skills level of the workforce, working practices which fall short of best practice standards and difficulties in raising capital to finance innovation or high technology projects. So what is the Government doing to ensure that the UK's scientific and innovative capability is exploited to the maximum extent possible?

There is no one 'magic model' we – or anyone else – can follow that will automatically reap all the benefits from basic scientific research. It is important to realize that there is no single type of company that can benefit from the outputs of the science and engineering base – all companies can. For example, many small companies do not cite the output of the science base, such as academic papers, as an important source of new product or process knowledge.

Figure 3 highlights this point. It seems to be internal company sources, supply chains and customer needs that are the main drivers of innovative activity. Yet the interesting, and illuminating, fact is that many of these firms employ science or engineering graduates. Figure 4 shows the relative statistics. The point is that those firms most likely to develop their own innovations and most receptive to new ideas and new technology are those with the highest proportion of graduates and qualified scientists and engineers.

As the report by the Science Policy Research Unit[3] shows, the
Science and Engineering Base influences companies in a variety of
ways. We need to recognize this when we are developing our
policies. In addition, policies which you might not immediately
think of as having an impact on the exploitation of science and
engineering base outputs can be important, such as training and

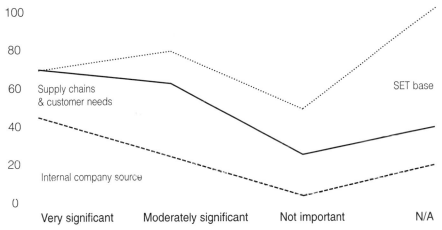

*Figure 3 Drivers of innovative ideas. (Source: DTI/IONS Survey of small
manufacturing companies)*

education policies and competition policies. In recent years the
Department of Trade and Industry (DTI) and the Office of
Science and Technology (OST) have pursued a range of coordinated and targeted policies, each designed to promote exploitation of science in different ways and in different areas.

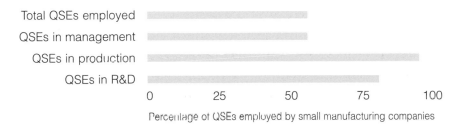

*Figure 4 Qualified Scientists and Engineers (QSEs) employed by small manu-
facturing companies. (Source: DTI/IONS Survey of small manufacturing companies)*

The Foresight Programme

The Foresight Programme, for example, aims to develop sustainable competitive advantage and an improved quality of life by bringing together business, the science base and government to identify and to respond to emerging opportunities in markets and technology. This Programme is carried forward by 16 Foresight Panels, each consisting of representatives of business, the scientific community and the public sector, and each addressing an important part of the UK's economic activity. There are, for instance, Panels focusing on financial services and retailing, as well as Panels on more traditional sectors such as chemicals and energy.

In addition to publishing reports identifying medium- and longer-term social, economic and market trends and the developments required in science and technology, the Programme has been active in encouraging the effective implementation of its recommendations.

Well over £350 million has now been committed to initiatives reflecting Foresight priorities. Seventeen new LINK programmes have been launched in response to Foresight, involving total funding of £148 million, to support pre-competitive collaborative research between business and the science and engineering base. The 1996 Foresight Challenge competition awarded £30 million to 24 consortia of business and the science base to undertake projects addressing Foresight priorities. A further £62 million was contributed by the private sector. Research Councils continue to align their spending plans to Foresight priorities where appropriate, introducing new initiatives as required.

In many of these activities Foresight has encouraged new partnerships between business and the science base. This and the ongoing work of the Foresight Panels helps to break down the boundaries between traditional sectors, allowing fresh ideas for innovative products and services to move more quickly into the marketplace. One excellent example is the Foresight-related Sector Challenge winner, the £1 million 'Tsunami' initiative, which brings together insurance companies and the British Antarctic Survey to improve the competitiveness of the UK insurance industry. The idea is to provide better information on areas of the country vulnerable to flooding or storm damage to insurance underwriters.

The LINK Collaborative Research Scheme
Another example is the LINK Collaborative Research Scheme which supports research partnerships between industry and the research base. Its aim has been to encourage industry and the research base to work together so that we reap the full benefits, in terms of improved industrial competitiveness and quality of life, of the knowledge, skills and expertise available in our universities – and to demonstrate to researchers that industrial research can be as challenging and fulfilling as academic research.

From modest beginnings in 1987, the LINK Programme has grown and developed to become the Government's principal mechanism for supporting industry/research base collaborations. It is now supported by seven Government Departments and five Research Councils, who offer up to 50 per cent funding for pre-competitive industrial research projects. The popularity and success of the scheme have led to a steady increase in government funding for LINK, with a spend of £33 million in 1997 – an amount more than equalled by industry. Fifty-seven LINK programmes have been announced since the scheme's launch, in areas as diverse as agriculture, electronics and information technology, biosciences, materials and engineering, representing a total government commitment of more than £280 million.

Because LINK projects involve pre-competitive research, companies will not normally see any immediate commercial benefit from participation. However, over the years an impressive array of new and improved products, services and processes have been developed as a result of LINK projects. Feedback from participating companies – over half of which are small or medium-sized businesses – clearly shows that they consider the benefits of LINK collaboration to be well worth the investment involved. And in many cases LINK collaborations have led to longer-term relationships between the universities and the companies involved.

Examples of LINK's achievements include the Renishaw Raman Imaging Spectrometer, which was developed with the help of a LINK project. It uses much lower-powered lasers than hitherto, enabling, for example, investigation of living cells without damaging the cell and the detection of minute quantities of drugs or explosives without destroying the forensic sample. In nanotechnology LINK supported developments include displacement transducers selected for the International Space Station; a focused ion beam tool for modifying microelectronic circuits; new production processes for ultrafine electroceramic powders; and an optical detection technique for single viruses. There are many other examples.

As it matures, each LINK programme produces a range of patents, new products and services, published research papers and new or improved scientific processes. One of LINK's major achievements, however, has been to help create a climate whereby industry and the research base are more willing and able to work together, to their mutual benefit and to the benefit of the UK economy as a whole.

The Teaching Company Scheme

One of the most effective ways to transfer technology and expertise from the science and engineering base to industry is via the movement and exchange of people. The Government therefore supports a number of activities which seek to encourage such collaborative partnerships, the most well known being TCS – the Teaching Company Scheme. This is a government-wide initiative, involving six Government Departments and five Research Councils. It helps companies to employ high quality graduates working for two years on a project which is central to its technology needs.

A review of TCS has shown that it has been exceptionally effective in stimulating innovation in industry and demonstrating to both the science base and industry the benefits of collaborative working agreements. Each million pounds of government grant for TCS programmes 'buys' all the following net cumulative additional activity: 58 jobs, £3.6 million value added, £13.3 million turnover, £3.0 million exports, £1.5 million capital expenditure and £0.2 million R&D expenditure. This last figure becomes more significant when you remember that 77 per cent of companies participating in TCS are small or medium-sized enterprises.

Other initiatives

In recent years the Research Councils have also made considerable efforts to increase the exploitation of their research, and those Councils responsible for institutes have established targets for them in terms of the amount of funding they gain from industry and other non-science base sources. For example, the Medical Research Council has established a number of mechanisms to exploit the intellectual property generated by its institutes, including a fund set up from licensing income to provide finance for very promising discoveries and an investment fund.

Another initiative being taken forward by the Engineering and Physical Sciences Research Council is the concept of Faraday Partnerships. These Partnerships build on the four so-called 'Faraday Principles' that have their origins in the work carried out by a working party on innovation established by HRH The Prince of Wales in 1991. Interactions between industry and the science base usually involve large companies. These large organizations are often well versed in how to go about such interactions, and do not require additional assistance from outside. But there are many smaller firms, at which Faraday Partnerships are aimed, who have little or no experience of interacting with the science base, but would benefit enormously from any assistance that might help them to do so. The first four Partnerships were announced in 1997 and will offer firms of all sizes an opportunity to work with key players – Higher Education Institutes, Research and Technology Organizations and other firms, who can add real value to a project in the broadest sense. By encouraging this wide networking we aim to build a more credible exploitation community between the science, engineering and technology base and business.

The Natural Environment Research Council has also recognized the benefits which could flow from better connections between the science base and potential users of the science base's research findings and expert knowledge. In partnership with others, including the University of Leeds, Natural Environment Research Council has piloted the development of a system called NEST – Network for the Exploitation of Science and Technology. In essence this makes use of the Worldwide Web environment to provide two way searching and communication between technology 'users' and 'suppliers'. A number of intermediate organizations, which play an important part in supporting small and medium-sized businesses are showing considerable interest and plans are being drawn up to fund and develop the pilot into a viable system.

Another policy which seeks to develop links in a different way is the Realising Our Potential Awards (ROPA) scheme, introduced as a pilot in 1994. The scheme addresses two issues. A deep and widespread culture of interaction between the science base and industry is recognized as being vital to the UK economic success but it is also recognized that researchers need the opportunity to explore new lines of investigation, lines which may lead to significant advances in the future. The process of making awards works by firstly allowing researchers who have received more than £25,000 in industry funding for basic and strategic research in the previous year to submit a ROPA research proposal to the Research Councils. Secondly, the proposal is judged, mainly on its feasibility and novelty.

The outcome of this approach is that ROPA projects tend to be seen as more 'risky' than conventional, fully peer-reviewed, Research Council funded projects. Researchers are also encouraged to work with industry so that they may be eligible to submit ROPA applications. Over 1200 ROPAs have been awarded with a value of

£108 million. Over £207 million of industrial funding was cited in these ROPA applications.

DTI also has a series of initiatives which aim to support the emerging biotechnology sector. These aim to improve exploitation of technology from the science base and to support the growth of young biotechnology companies by providing management expertise and financial advice. For example, the Biotechnology Mentoring and Incubator Challenge aims to encourage the provision of incubators and specialist business mentoring services to help young biotechnology companies grow. Winners are offered up to £500,000 towards the cost of a demonstrator project. Another initiative is the Biotechnology Exploitation Platforms Challenge, which aims to improve the management of intellectual property (IP) in the bioscience base. It encourages syndicates of academic institutions with complementary technology to build partnerships with intermediaries who can offer the necessary specialist skills in marketing and IP management of technology. Winning syndicates are granted 50 per cent of eligible costs up to £250,000.

DTI is also sponsoring independent financial consultants to provide a UK Biotechnology Finance Advisory Service. The aim of the service is to assist both existing biotechnology companies and individuals or organizations forming new companies to access appropriate forms of finance. The service, which is free of charge, assists by identifying potential sources of private sector funds and appropriate government grants. It also signposts other assistance available through the network of advice centres for small and medium-sized enterprises and other sources, and improves communication between biotechnology companies and different providers of finance.

Evidence of improvement

There have been signs of a turn around and that industry is increasingly looking to the science and engineering base as a source of new ideas. For example, the evidence is that industry is increasingly collaborating with research establishments and institutes. Between 1981 and 1994 joint publications increased from just under 500 to around 1400. Between August 1994 and July 1995 some 46 new companies 'span out' from Higher Education Establishments. The CBI/NatWest Innovation Trends survey reported that 73 per cent of manufacturing and 80 per cent of non-manufacturing CBI members collaborated with academics during 1996.[4] Another indicator is the links that exist between industry and universities: some 40 per cent of universities run industry clubs and 75 per cent run courses for industry.

The future
What lessons can we learn from the past and what policies need to be put in place to enable us to profit – in all senses of the word – from the discoveries and inventions of the future? Innovation and the effective use of technology will continue to be key factors in sustaining and enhancing the competitiveness and economic performance of the UK in the twenty-first century. They will also play a vital role in improving the future quality of all our lives.

We will need policies to capture the creativity of both individuals and of business, and to help them to prove the potential value of their ideas and translate them into innovations. One such policy is the Government's proposal to establish a National Endowment for Science, Technology and the Arts (NESTA). National Lottery funds are to be used to yield up to £14 million per year, which an Independent Board of Trustees will allocate. This money should help talented individuals to develop their full potential in the creative industries, and help turn creativity and ideas into products or services.

Another area in which a great deal has been achieved in recent years is bringing undergraduates and postgraduates into contact with industry, and vice versa. An excellent example is the Young Entrepreneurs Scheme sponsored by the Biotechnology and Biological Sciences Research Council and business, through which undergraduate and postgraduate teams compete to present a business plan for a hypothetical start-up company based on their research. The enthusiasm, and proficiency, which the competition generates are truly extraordinary. Initiatives of this kind must multiply and endure if UK industry – which in the end is the same as the people in it – is ever to become as research-receptive as I believe it must.

We also need to look at rewarding researchers for the transfer of their skills and knowledge to the users of these things. There are many ways of providing the reward, as there are of making the transfer. Some are more or less spontaneous – for example, academics who have 'spun off' and started up small companies from their university research teams. Sometimes the developments have been due to subtle – and occasionally perhaps not so subtle – contextualization by Government. There is nothing wrong in that. We need to be looking for further incentives. We are still far from the point where development of research is seen as second nature, and not as some kind of embarrassing aberration. The recommendations from the Dearing Inquiry[5], and now the Government response, are providing a fresh impetus in this direction.

It will be equally important to continue to encourage both businesses and individuals, although it is for business itself to create the new and improved products and services which customers will want to buy. The government role is likely to include activities which:

- encourage firms to innovate and take the long term view;
- encourage partnerships and networks to spread best practice in science, technology and the business process;
- and help individual firms to acquire the skills and know-how which will enable them to adapt to and profit from future market changes and technological developments.

We are now able to think about the next phase of the Foresight Programme, which will be designed to produce fresh and updated findings in the autumn of the year 2000. The Office of Science and Technology has published a consultation paper on the future of Foresight. Responding to Ministers' wishes to increase the profile of quality of life issues in the Programme, we are trying to encourage wider participation. Thus scientists' and technologists' views are considered together with contributions from, for example, young people, old people, disadvantaged people, and people who have views on future behaviour patterns in these sorts of groups. In this way the Programme will try to understand better the changing markets of the future, both at home and overseas.

Through this process we will also be trying to establish new networks between groups that might otherwise not interact effectively. Since this has been one of the enduring achievements of the Programme to date, and is highly valued by those involved, the next phase may well include effective networking as a specific objective. This is because through such networks ideas travel between sectors, and more quickly, giving organizations competitive advantage through improved innovation, and the ability to react more quickly to opportunities and threats as they emerge. In this way, the Programme will help to ensure that UK science will be able to continue to make a valuable contribution to future economic and social progress.

The Foresight LINK Awards, a competition for which £10 million of public funds has been made available – to be at least matched by businesses – was announced by the President of the Board of Trade in 1997. The Awards are intended to provide a fresh stimulus to public–private sector partnerships, particularly in Foresight priority areas and in sectors which have a comparatively less well-established track record of collaboration between businesses and the research base. The priority areas are a cleaner world, social shaping and the impact of new technology and precision and control in management.

One important factor that has limited the UK's commercial exploitation of research and technological inventions is Intellectual

Property (IP). However, researchers in our academic institutions are now becoming much more aware of the importance of IP. They understand the need to safeguard their discoveries to enable the future commercialization of the product. The Government's schemes to promote innovation and foster partnerships between the science base and industry place a strong emphasis on the need to protect any intellectual property arising from the project being supported. The Patent Office make considerable efforts to convince all potential patentees of the importance of IP. The DTI, together with the Economic and Social Research Council and the Intellectual Property Institute, is also sponsoring a £1 million research programme on IP. We believe these activities can only help to improve the nation's understanding of the relationship between IP and commercial success.

One of the UK's strongest assets is the inventiveness and creativity of its people. We must continue to encourage the conversion of that creativity into products and services that will generate wealth and improved quality of life for the UK in years to come.

References

1   Schumpeter, J.A. (1942), *Essays: on entrepreneurs, innovations, business cycles and the evolution of capitalism.*
2   *Supporting Research and Development to Promote Economic Growth: The Federal Government's Role* (1995), a report prepared by The Council of Economic Advisers, USA.
3   SPRU (1995), *Changing Shape of British Science,* Falmer, Sussex: Science Policy Research Unit.
4   *CBI/NatWest Innovation Trends Survey* (annual).
5   Dearing, Sir R. (1997), *Higher Education in the Learning Society,* The National Committee of Inquiry into Higher Education.

The Decline (and Success) of Science in England

Dr Simon Schaffer

Reader in History and Philosophy of Science, University of Cambridge

This title is taken from *Reflections on the Decline of Science in England and on some of its Causes*, written in 1830 by Charles Babbage, then Lucasian Professor of Mathematics at Cambridge, promoter of a new, high-powered calculating engine and one of the nation's most notable scientific reformers. This was Babbage's slogan:

> In England, particularly with respect to the more difficult and abstract sciences, we are much below other nations, not merely of equal rank, but below several even of inferior power.[1]

He was scandalized

> that a country eminently distinguished for its mechanical and manufacturing ingenuity should be indifferent to the progress of enquiries which form the highest departments of that knowledge on whose more elementary truths its wealth and rank depend.[1]

The research system and economics
Babbage included a remarkable passage on the various ways in which corruption could spread even to the everyday work of science. He categorized hoaxes, designed to twit scientific authority: forgery, a hoax designed to deceive everybody for ever; trimming, where the scientist claimed excessive observational

accuracy; and what he called cookery, where a huge quantity of data was used as a reservoir from which a desirable result could be cunningly extracted.

What should interest us more in the work is Babbage's acute analysis of the tension between the economic facts of the market and the system by which research could be encouraged. He adhered to the virtues of the division of labour and the role which market price should play in the encouragement of the factory system, but in his analysis of English scientific decline he immediately recognized that market economics would seem to rule against any need for distinctive public encouragement of inventors:

> The public who consume the new commodity or profit by the new invention, are much better judges of its merit than the government can be; the reward which arises from the sale of the commodity is usually much larger than that which government would be justified in bestowing; and it is exactly proportioned to the consumption, that is, to the want which the public feel for the new article.[2]

Yet Babbage simultaneously understood that if profit were the only system by which inventors were rewarded, then no mechanism could be devised for rewarding those who developed the purer, more abstract principles on which, eventually, such commercially viable schemes always depended. It was necessary to have some provision, inevitably publicly funded, for the secluded enquiries on which the arts always ultimately depended.

Under current conditions, Babbage reckoned, 'scarcely any man can be expected to pursue abstract science unless he possess a private fortune, and unless he can resolve to give up all intention of improving it'. We can see exactly the source of Babbage's argument here – the view that true science is (and should be) insulated from social and commercial pressure, that pure enquiry long precedes technological development and that true scientists are an exceptional race. Scientific heroes on this showing would be treated as supreme achievers and thus be ranked in ever more carefully constructed tables of merit.

Invention and genius

There were specific features of Babbage's work which fomented the insulated, individualist story of scientific invention. Until the early nineteenth century the standard model of invention's sources was profoundly collectivist. Protagonists of enlightened science such as Joseph Priestley had always argued that discovery and invention were not due to specially privileged individuals but rather to widespread and small-scale local labour. Francis Bacon had taught there was even a method for making discoveries which all of good will could learn. The term 'genius' was rarely applied to men of science. Since their work, if reliable, must be replicable by others, they could scarcely be granted the title of original creators. None could recompose Hamlet, it was argued, but anyone could, in theory, rederive the principles of celestial mechanics.

What happened during Babbage's lifetime was the development of the notion of genius and its application specifically to scientists. Against this heroic campaign were the apostles of necessity, the mother of invention. For such men campaigning for abolition of the patent laws, such as Isambard Kingdom Brunel, 'really good improvements are not the result of inspiration; they are not, strictly speaking, inventions.' Brunel and his allies urged that innovations 'result from a demand which circumstances happen to create.'[3]

Among the campaigners against the patent system was the radical artisan Thomas Hodgskin, an interlocutor and political rival of Babbage, for whom the direction of science and invention was determined not by unique heroes but by the innumerable labours of fellow-artisans. According to Hodgskin, this gave workmen the right over machinery they designed, not the masters, and this would tell against the ideology of genius. This, then, provided the intellectual and political setting of Babbage's declinism. By insisting on the rights of genius he clearly posed the new problem of the best way of rewarding these almost completely disembodied minds whose social location was so obscure.

Some philosophers of science are still impressed by the distinction between the life-world of our ordinary experience and the abstract, rational universe of the natural sciences. The scientists who ply their trade in such a world are seen to be unlike anyone else, not merely or even mainly because of their training. Much is made of the specific moral features of the scientific community, its intolerance of fraud, bias or vice, its unique methods for securing reliable and effective knowledge, and its capacity to settle matters of dispute and interest. Many emphasize the sciences' difference from any other means humans have ever devised for finding out about their world. Such views imply that the institutions of the sciences have, or at least should have, the function of preserving scientific activity from external prejudices and influences.

Scientific seclusion

In general, scientific institutions are surrounded by systems of seclusion. Modern science parks help to reinforce something like a rural setting for the scientific laboratory. This imagery of rural retreat has a long history. The urban, urbane scholars of medieval universities were displaced by the courtly, courteous humanists of the Renaissance countryside. Think of all the stories which surround heroic scientists with anecdotes of absent-mindedness and quasi-monastic asceticism.

But inside such labs the industrialization and casualization of the scientific workforce proceeds apace. It is as though knowledge is made in what the architect Thomas Markus has called 'production utopias', where careful isolation secures a peculiarly invulnerable social order entirely separated from the existing host culture. The image of the production utopia supports the idea that we can understand the history of the sciences without thinking about the organization of scientific workers and without thinking very much about the institutions where their work is performed.

There are two reasons why this idea is false. First, the claim that science goes on in guarded privacy is itself certainly a public claim. Seclusion makes sense only in relation to a wider society. Second, in order to make reliable natural knowledge, scientists have to import and export quantities of people, artefacts and information. A truly isolated institution could never produce any reliable knowledge.

Supporting science
This brings us back to Babbage. Faced with the belief that true science must stay pure and insulated it was hard to see how to support it and how to recruit financial and political resources to secure its continued existence. The key lay in redefining the very notion of intellectual property to do justice to the condition of English science. Babbage noted that farmland was patrimony, a temporary inheritance, whose productivity was scarcely our own creation. Yet English law, more than anything else, institutional-ized exclusive individual property in land as part of its ultimate rejection of the moral economy. Why not do so for scientific inventions?

'Two courses are open to those individuals who are thus endowed with nature's wealth,' Babbage explained.

> They may lock up in their own bosoms the mysteries they have penetrated, and by applying their knowledge to the production of some substance in demand in commerce, thus minister to the wants or comforts of their species, while they reap in pecuniary profit the legitimate reward of their exertions.[4]

The patent system adequately compensated the latter. But what of scientists?

> It is open to them, on the other hand, to disclose the secret they have torn from nature and by allowing mankind to participate with them to claim at once that splendid

reputation which is rarely refused to the inventors of valuable discoveries in the arts of life.[4]

Here was the nub. Mere reputation might not be enough to keep English scientists at work. More was necessary to save the nation's intellectual progress.

Location and progress

The insistence that science properly occupies a place entirely separate from the social and technological order makes it hard to define the place the sciences ought to have within that order. The imagery of decline – and its correlative of public ignorance of the sciences or even hostility to them – thus perversely trades on the equally pervasive imagery of seclusion. We should move our attention, therefore, from issues of chronology (progress, decline) to those of geography (location, resources, place).

The vocabulary of space and technique provides a powerful resource in rethinking the predicament of the cultivation of scientific and technological invention. For a long time public discourse on the sciences in England has been obsessed by temporality. We ask about our heroic ancestors, precursors, anticipations; we are told of scientists who were somehow ahead of their time, who saw the future. A genius is someone who derives a truth before the evidence is in, but whose veracity is born out by the future. Most tellingly, perhaps, we debate the possibility that the sciences, especially physics or cognitive science, may be reaching an end, or may instead soon be revolutionized.

It is in these terms that declinism flourishes, not least since the international comparisons of short-term achievements on which Babbage and his allies traded stay omnipresent in modish imagery of competitiveness and enterprise. As a utopia, so nowhere, and an ideal, so immaterial, science has been hard to see as a materially embodied enterprise with its own geography, its personnel and institutions having their own vitally important layout and location.

London in Babbage's day

Babbage's career provides a superb and telling example of such a geography. London in the 1820s and 1830s was a fractured world. South of the river, in the industrial suburb of Lambeth, were the workshops of the machinists whose labours drove the production of automatic tools and accurate design. In the plush milieu of the West End, genteel Londoners could witness shows of the triumphs of these new machine systems in public lectures and carefully orchestrated museums. Here, too, were the wardens of scientific reason, the Astronomical Society, the Royal Society, the Royal Institution.

Northwards again, in the fashionable houses of Marylebone, lived men such as Babbage and Charles Darwin, ambitious reformers who sought to rethink human nature in the name of a reconstructed scientific and social order. Fashionable parties drew mixtures of gentlemen of science and lords of fashion in a common culture. In the north-east were the huge working-class districts, areas where Babbage in 1832 sought to run for parliament.

This is the geography of Babbage's intelligence, the world where his systematic vision was forged. His projects were certainly dependent on the city's workshops and on government offices but they were also tangled up with the culture of the West End, brightly lit shops and showrooms, front-of-house hucksters and backroom impresarios. Babbage's influential pessimism about the decline of science in England is best understood not as a badly informed commentary on the historical development of English scientific achievement but rather as a remark about the breakdown of co-ordination between these crucial but sundered zones of London science.

The reorientation is more telling when we recognize the startling fact that each nineteenth-century debate about the position of the sciences in English society was phrased in just the declinist terms Babbage laid down. In the 1850s spokesmen for English science sought major changes in the organization of the universities to aid national economic performance against the threat of decadence. In 1873 Norman Lockyer's new magazine, *Nature*, judged 'science all but dead in England'.[5] In 1880 Thomas Huxley lectured at Birmingham that

> one has reason to observe that no reply to a troublesome argument tells so well as calling its author a mere scientific specialist. And I am afraid that it is not permissible to speak of this form of opposition to scientific education in the past tense.[5]

It is no argument to suggest that such doom was and is mistaken simply because it is both recurrent and precedented. It is legitimate to diagnose the tone of voice as a symptom of a peculiar predicament with which science has been faced – the matched insistence that it be valued by society and that its intimate activity has no place within that society.

Scientists as saints

My diagnosis would wish to complement a vocabulary of disembodied heroes with the techniques of geography, to help define better the places and spaces of the sciences as well as their saints and martyrs.

Alongside such endeavours we could proffer a spatial model of the sciences, insist that they are distributed activities involving the labours of many in carefully organized institutions linked by powerful and often visible networks of skill, practice and hardware. For geology and natural history, physics and engineering, the spatially extended networks of nineteenth-century Britain were decisive resources and determining influences. The case of physics and technology is scarcely different. The Empire relied on cable telegraphy undersea, its very nerve system. For the cable system to work, reliable electromagnetic standards were needed. The demand for these standards led directly to the establishment of a host of teaching laboratories in British universities and, even more decisively, to the development of the dynamic field theory of electromagnetism by Maxwell and Kelvin from the 1850s. Whereas other countries, such as Germany and France, could rely on overhead lines, the British needed submarine telegraphy. This is why the British developed such a powerful new physical theory and why, elsewhere in Europe, more conventional models stayed fashionable.

In a radio programme the former editor of *Nature*, John Maddox, delivered a fascinating attack on heroism:

> There are many occasions in the past 50 years when one can see how a relatively small contribution by a person who does not win a Nobel prize, who does not get lauded around the streets of New York, is in fact of crucial importance to the development of science. It is one of the moving things about the scientific enterprise now that it depends crucially on the contributions of the pygmies as well as the giants.[6]

What Maddox says may be right but it is not new. What he calls the pygmies have always been crucial. Science is a set of embodied activities whose geographical emplacement is decisive and which therefore permeates society.

Challenging education

What are the best means for promoting invention and emulation on this less hagiographic picture? This is a challenge to educators, who have indeed long sought to understand and represent work in the sciences as a pervasive aspect of common life. Think, for example, of the remarkable work of 1980s and 1990s Cornell ornithologists who, by linking together large-scale networks of North American birdwatchers, children and adults, have begun producing radical new models of bird migration and distribution and simultaneously taught their society about the methods and assumptions, techniques and forms of argument, of the best form of science.

The mobilization of local activists stays a decisive resource for the institutions of spatial science, and here museums and exhibitions have a crucial role to play. Thus current insistence on the amorality of the sciences is pernicious and flows directly from a mistaken faith in the notion that the cloister is the last best hope of pure knowledge. Precisely because scientists themselves might wish to defend, contest or redirect the ways of scientific invention, it must be the case that a certain kind of moral engagement is crucial to the decline or success of science in England.

Science and politics

A hundred years ago Alfred Russell Wallace produced one of the most important analyses of science's place in society. His book, *The Wonderful Century*, was second to none in its lauding of the progress of science in England. In just under a century, Wallace pointed out, the country had seen radical technical change: rail and steam ships, telegraphy and the telephone, electric light and photography, anaesthesia and antisepsis, the phonograph and X-rays.

In a manner familiar to today's exponents of millennialism, Wallace matched technical changes with advances in the sciences: energy conservation and kinetic theory, the periodic table and the theory of evolution, cell theory and embryology. What past age could compare? In the same breath he issued a dire warning. This was his new version of declinism. Having first worked as a surveyor on the Welsh borders during the ferocious agricultural riots against enclosure of the 1840s, learned socialism first hand in the Midlands, then applied the lessons of social conflict and biogeography to his experiences in the East Indies, Wallace was well placed to see how the spaces of science and politics were entangled. Instead of wrongheadedly bemoaning the neglect of science by his society, he carefully diagnosed the ills and threats that the wrong kind of science and politics had produced.

Almost all of Wallace's complaints now seem, to put it mildly, equally deluded. He complained that scientists had wrongly neglected phrenology and psychical research and he bewailed the introduction of compulsory vaccination. Above all, he alleged:

we have yet so sinfully mismanaged our social economy as to give unprecedented and injurious luxury to the few, while millions are compelled to suffer a lifelong deficiency of the barest necessities for a healthy existence. Instead of devoting these highest powers of our greatest men to remedy these evils, we see governments of the most advanced nations arming their people to the teeth, and expending much of their wealth and all the resources of their science, in preparation for the destruction of life, of property and of happiness.[7]

Does this sound as out of touch as Wallace's admittedly idiosyncratic attitude to spiritualism and vaccination? Rather than the declinism launched in 1830 by Babbage, which was posited on an insulation of science from the social economy, we need this other kind of critique which, by insisting on the role which science plays in our own society, gives us much hope for truly inventive progress.

References

1   Babbage, C. (1830) *Reflections on the Decline of Science in England*, p. 1, London: Fellowes.
2   Ibid, p.13.
3   Cited in MacLeod, C. (1995) 'Concepts of Invention and the Patent Controversy in Victorian Britain' in *Technological Change* (ed. Robert Fox), pp. 147, London: Harwood Academic.
4   Babbage, C. *Reflections on the Decline of Science in England*, p. 132 (see above).
5   Cited in Alter, P. (1987) *The Reluctant Patron: Science and the State in Britain 1850–1920*, p. 215, Oxford: Berg.
6   Cited in Bragg, M. (ed.) (1998) *On giants' shoulders*, p. 358, London: Hodder and Stoughton.
7   Wallace, A. R. (1899) *The Wonderful Century: Its Successes and Its Failures*, Third Edition, p. 377, London: Swan Sonnenschein.

INFORMATION ON RSA
PROGRAMMES

The RSA's programmes focus primarily on business and industry, design and technology, education, the arts and the environment. Projects, which range from campaigns and enquiries, sometimes leading to a publication, to award schemes are largely self-funded with money coming from a variety of sources including trusts, foundations, companies and government. Some projects develop and grow to such an extent as to warrant independent status and they become 'spin-off' organizations. Examples include the RSA Examinations Board, Centre for Tomorrow's Company, Campaign for Learning and National Advisory Council for Careers and Educational Guidance (NACCEG).

Current RSA projects include:

THE ARTS MATTER PROGRAMME

This is a series of projects focused on arts education including:

- The Effect and Effectiveness of Arts Education in Secondary Schools

  A three-year research project with the National Foundation for Educational Research documenting the range of effects and outcomes of a school-based arts education. (Publication: *The Effects and Effectiveness of Arts Education in Schools - NFER, interim report, 1998*)

- The Arts in Initial Teacher Training

  A research project documenting and assessing the current situation and future trends with respect to arts experience in the training and development of teachers. (Publication: *The Disappearing Arts?* 1998)

- Arts Audit

  A pilot project developed in Bristol to assist schools in the undertaking of an arts audit. A practical guide is available. (Publication: *Investing in the Arts*, 1998)

- Other arts publications

  Guaranteeing an entitlement to the Arts in schools, 1995; *The Arts Matter* - series of lectures, published by Gower, 1997; *Work, creativity and the arts*, 1999.

Contact: Michaela Crimmin, Head of Arts, RSA

THE ART FOR ARCHITECTURE AWARD SCHEME
This scheme encourages cross-disciplinary approaches to building and landscape projects by providing funds for artists to work as part of a design team. The emphasis is on collaboration, enabling artists to play a significant role in the initial stages of a project.

Contact: Jes Fernie, Project Manager, Art for Architecture, RSA

STUDENT DESIGN AWARDS
The Student Design Awards scheme has, over the last 75 years, become the UK's premier competition for student designers, attracting over 3,000 entries a year for over 40 realistic and challenging briefs. The scheme encourages good practice, innovation, sustainability and responsible design solutions. (Publications: *Student Design Awards Projects* book, 1998/99; *Student Design Awards Blueprint Review*, 1997/98; *Design for Ageing Network Teaching Pack*, 1996)

Contact: Susan Hewer, Head of Design, RSA

REDEFINING SCHOOLING
This project calls for a re-engineering of the education system as a whole and is working to develop the framework of a new competence-based National Curriculum. It follows on from the recent Redefining Work project, a two-year national debate on how patterns of work are changing and the impact of these changes. (Publications: *Redefining Schooling* discussion paper, 1998; *Redefining Work* report, 1998, available from Gower)

Contact: Lesley James, Head of Education, RSA

PROJECT2001
Project2001 opens the door to qualifications for people of any age who have built up skills and competencies through experience in the voluntary sector either as volunteers or paid employees. It also offers mentors to managers in participating voluntary organizations. (Publication: *Qualified by Experience*, 1998)

Contact: Janet Fleming, Project Director, Project 2001, RSA

FOCUS ON FOOD
This project is run by the RSA at Dean Clough, Halifax. It is a five-year campaign aiming to promote, develop and sustain the place of food in education.

Contact: Anita Cormac, Project Director, Focus on Food, RSA at Dean Clough (tel 01422 250250)

FORUM FOR ETHICS IN THE WORKPLACE
The Forum for Ethics in the Workplace seeks to develop high ethical standards at work. Set up in 1997 and funded by the Comino Foundation, the Forum meets regularly, bringing together a wide variety of professionals to discuss ethics in the context of work.

Contact: Susie Harries, Project Administrator, Forum for Ethics in the Workplace, RSA

OTHER CONTACTS
RSA Examinations Board (OCR)
Tel 01203 470033

The Centre for Tomorrow's Company
Mark Goyder, Director
Centre for Tomorrow's Company
Tel 0171 930 5150

Campaign for Learning
Bill Lucas, Director
Campaign for Learning
Tel 0171 930 1111

National Advisory Council for Careers and Educational Guidance
(NACCEG)
Tel 01962 878340

INDEX